SEW EASY
EMBELLISHMENTS

Nancy Zieman

Oxmoor
House.

Sew Easy Embellishments

by Nancy Zieman
from the "Sewing with Nancy" series
©1997 by Nancy Zieman and Oxmoor House, Inc.
Book Division of Southern Progress Corporation
P.O. Box 2463, Birmingham, Alabama 35201

Published by Oxmoor House, Inc., and Leisure Arts, Inc.

Library of Congress Catalog Number: 97-66727
Hardcover ISBN: 0-8487-1537-3
Softcover ISBN: 0-8487-1605-1
Manufactured in the United States of America
First Printing 1997

Editor-in-Chief: Nancy Fitzpatrick Wyatt
Senior Crafts Editor: Susan Ramey Cleveland
Senior Editor, Editorial Services: Olivia Kindig Wells
Art Director: James Boone

Sew Easy Embellishments

Editor: Lois Martin
Editorial Assistant: Cecile Y. Nierodzinski
Copy Editor: Anne S. Dickson
Designer: Emily Albright Parrish
Associate Art Director: Cindy Cooper
Production and Distribution Director: Phillip Lee
Associate Production Manager: Theresa L. Beste
Senior Photographer: John O'Hagan
Photo Stylists: Katie Stoddard, Linda Baltzell Wright
Illustrator: Rochelle Stibb
Editorial Assistance, Nancy's Notions: Betty Hanneman

We're Here for You!

We at Oxmoor House are dedicated to serving you with reliable information that expands your imagination and enriches your life. We welcome your comments and suggestions.
Please write us at:
Oxmoor House, Inc.
Editor, *Sew Easy Embellishments*
2100 Lakeshore Drive
Birmingham, AL 35209
To order additional publications, call 1-205-877-6560.

The editor thanks Allison D. Ingram for modeling the fashions in this book, Ann Marie Harvey for providing hands to photograph, and Mark McDowell of the Sewing Machine Mart in Homewood, Alabama, for lending the Pfaff sewing machines and sergers used in photography.

A Note from Nancy

Nancy Zieman, author, teacher, and business-woman, hosted her 15th season of "Sewing With Nancy" on the Public Broadcasting System in 1997.

If you're like me, one of the reasons you love sewing is that you can create one-of-a-kind garments and gifts. Discovering the right fabric to go with the perfect pattern is fun, but I find it even more satisfying to create a special embellishment that sets my project apart.

Sometimes, I need an embellishment I can stitch quickly and easily, adding it to a garment I've bought. When I have more time, I may create my own fabric or use my sewing machine to add silk-ribbon embroidery to a stitching project.

If you've never thought of yourself as a fashion designer, here's a chance to release your creativity! Just choose a technique from this book that looks like it would be fun for you, and gather your supplies and fabric. Take your time, and enjoy the sewing. You be the designer!

Contents

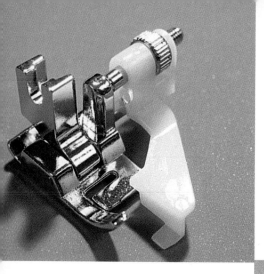

A built-in guide on the blindhem foot *(left and page 12)* keeps seam width even. Choosing the right thread *(right and page 14)* makes any project easier to stitch. ▶

Beginning with the right tools simplifies embellishing. From thread to presser feet to scissors, creative supplies enhance your sewing.

Creative Supplies

◀ A notch in the blade of buttonhole scissors *(left and page 9)* helps you cut precise openings. For a novel edge, try a pinking or a wave blade in your rotary cutter *(right and page 9).* ▶

◀ Magnetic templates for a buttonhole foot *(left and page 12)* ensure that buttonholes are just the size needed.

Confetti Appliqué,
page 47

Specialized Notions

Choose from a wide assortment of tools and notions that make sewing easier.

Bamboo Pointer & Creaser

Use the pointed end to turn collars, cuffs, lapels, or appliqués. Flip the tool over and use the curved, beveled end to temporarily press seams open.

Bias Tape Maker

Slip a bias strip into the wide end of this metal tool and pull the strip out as you press. You create single-fold bias tape with edges that are always uniform. Bias tape makers are available in a wide range of widths, from 6 mm to 50 mm.

Bodkin

This tweezerlike notion has special teeth that grasp your fabric or trim, making it easier for you to draw lace, ribbon, and elastic through a casing. Also handy for weaving.

Collar Point & Tube Turner

Turn lapel and collar points, pocket flaps, spaghetti straps, and belts using this scissorlike tool.

Fasturn®

Used for turning fabric tubes right side out, this specialty notion has two sections: a metal cylinder and a wire hook. Place a fabric tube over the cylinder, and use the hook to pull the fabric through the inside of the cylinder, turning the tube right side out. (See page 106 for diagrams of how to use this notion.) Also inserts cording.

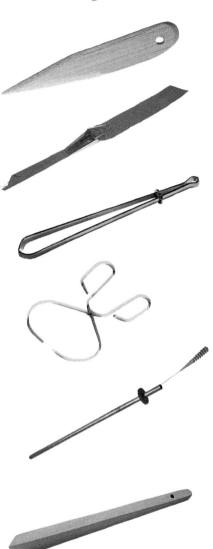

Little Wooden Iron

A unique finger-pressing notion, this smoothly sanded hardwood tool is useful for opening seams and for pressing seams to the side when quilting. Choose a right- or left-handed iron, since the tool's pressing edge is made at an angle. The 5¼"-long (13 cm-long) Little Wooden Iron has a comfortable grasp.

Seam Sealant

Products like Fray Check™ and No-Fray reinforce and lock threads to prevent fraying of seams. Stabilize buttonholes with a drop of this clear-drying liquid.

Stiletto

Use this awl-like tool to ease fabric, lace, or ribbon under the presser foot as you sew or quilt. A stiletto also helps keep seam allowances in place as you stitch, straighten silk ribbon embroidery stitches, and turn appliqué points.

Cutting Tools

Choosing the right cutting tool gets your project off to a good start.

Appliqué Scissors

Use appliqué scissors for trimming close to edgestitching. The scissors' large bill lifts the fabric to be trimmed, and the curved handles ensure a comfortable hand position.

Buttonhole Cutter and Block

This tool helps you make neat, professional-looking buttonholes. The cutter has a hardwood handle with a hardened steel blade; the block comes in various shapes. Place the buttonhole over the block and cut with the cutter. If the buttonhole is smaller than the cutter, place half the buttonhole over the edge of the block, cut, and repeat for the second part.

Buttonhole Scissors

These handy scissors allow you to make precise buttonhole cuts. Adjust the screw at the handle of the scissors to hold them in a partially open position. This allows you to use part of the blade to make precise ½" to ¼" (1.3 cm to 3.8 cm) buttonhole cuts. Fabric in front of the buttonhole bunches safely in the reservoir at the base of the blade.

Dressmaker Shears

The term "shears" refers to blades of 8" or longer. Shears are available with or without bent handles. Use them for general sewing needs.

Pinking Shears

These shears with sawtooth edges cut decorative, ravel-resistant edges of seams and trim. When you cut curved seam allowances with pinking shears, you automatically reduce bulk in the finished seam.

Rotary Cutter

This special fabric cutting tool looks and works like a pizza cutter. Easy to grasp and comfortable to use, a rotary cutter has a round sharp blade attached to the end of a handle. The replaceable blades come with straight, wavy, or pinked edges. Rotary cutters were developed for quilting, since they can cut through several layers of fabric at once, but they're useful for other types of sewing as well.

Rotary Cutting Mat

Designed for use with rotary cutters, these mats protect your work surface and provide guides to make cutting straight edges and identical pieces fast and easy. The mat's cutting side is printed with hash marks every ¼", a 1" grid, and diagonal lines to help you cut triangles. The mats are sold in various sizes. Store mats flat to prevent warping.

Marking Tools

Top-quality sewing requires accuracy. The right marking tools will help you achieve it.

Chalk

This oil-free marking tool is available in several forms.
- A chalk wheel accurately transfers markings to fabric with a fine line of chalk. Fill the wheel with loose white chalk (for dark fabrics) or blue chalk (for light fabrics).
- Triangle Tailor's Chalk has a chalk base in a firm triangular form, and never leaves a stain. Use it to make crisp, accurate lines on all your sewing projects. Triangle Tailor's Chalk comes in red, yellow, white, and blue.
- A Soapstone Fabric Marker will not harm fabrics because it's made from natural soapstone. Soapstone marks are clearly visible, yet rub off easily when no longer needed. It does not show up on light-colored fabrics. This marker is adjustable and sharpens in a pencil sharpener.

Fabric Marking Pen

This pinpoint pen marks fine lines so you can trace small designs or mark complex patterns clearly. Fabric marking pens are available in air- and water-soluble form.
- The Wonder Marker's blue ink disappears with just a drop of water, making it a perfect marking tool to use on washable fabrics.

> ### Note from Nancy
> *Always test fabric markers on a scrap of the fabric you plan to use to be sure the marks come out. And remember that heat will set these marks. Remove the marks before pressing, and do not use hot water to remove water-soluble marks.*

Fabric Marking Pencil

A super-thin lead pencil specifically designed for fabric, the fabric marking pencil is always sharp. Since it contains less graphite than a standard pencil, it resists smearing and washes out beautifully.

Gridded Paper

An iron-on paper with a ¼" grid, this paper bonds permanently to other paper and temporarily to fabric (without leaving a residue). Gridded paper is ideal for appliqué and stencilling.

Hot Tape™

No more pins or burned fingers as you position transfers, appliqué, and pleats! Hot Tape is an adhesive-backed, gridded tape that's heat resistant. Use it to create pleats or position appliqué. The tape peels off easily without any residue and may be reused. Note: Do not sew over tape because it gums up the needle.

Pattern Transfer Materials

Use a traditional sawtoothed tracing wheel and tracing/transfer paper to mark seam lines, trace quilting patterns, indicate appliqué positions, and more. The paper is reusable, wax-free, and carbonless, and marks from it erase, sponge off, or wash out. Tracing/transfer paper comes in a variety of colors.

• Pressure-fax® Transfer Pen & Paper is simple to use: just trace and rub. Use a transfer pen to trace your design onto the special paper. Then simply place the paper (image side down) over your fabric and rub with your fingernail, a spoon, or the Little Wooden Iron.

• The Fabric Pattern Transfer Kit™ includes everything you need to transfer silk-ribbon embroidery designs to fabric. Trace a design onto the transfer paper and place the traced design over fabric. Use the purple pen tip to retrace the design, which marks your fabric. The pen has a white tip to erase marks.

Pigma Permanent Marker

These pens work best on natural, untreated 100% cotton or cotton blends, where their marks dry quickly and will not fade, smear, or feather when dry. Pigma ink is waterproof. Use these pens to personalize heirloom treasures and draw details on projects.

Measuring Tools

For clothes to fit, quilts to go together without bunching, and home decorating projects to cover surfaces, you must measure carefully when you cut.

Quilting Rulers

These heavy-duty, clear acrylic rulers were developed for quilters to use with rotary cutters, but they're also useful in other sewing projects. Quilting rulers come in various sizes. The most popular ones are listed below.

• A 1" x 6" pocket-size ruler is convenient and versatile for quilting and sewing.

• Keep a 1" x 12½" ruler for quick measuring references.

• The larger 3" x 18" ruler is great for secondary cutting and for fine patchwork techniques. Use positions clearly marked on the ruler to cut accurate 30°, 45°, and 60° angles.

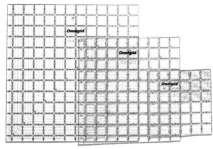

Quilting Squares

Quilting squares help you square-up quilt blocks. (See Crazy Patchwork with Decorative Stitching on page 68.) The squares come in 6", 9½", and 12½", and are marked with diagonal bias lines.

Half Squares

Use Half Squares to cut half-square triangles up to 8" in size.

Sewing Machine Feet

Matching the right presser foot to the job can save you hours of sewing time and simplify many stitching jobs.

Blindhem Foot

The blindhem foot is one of the most versatile presser feet in your accessory box. In addition to its traditional use for hemming woven and knit fabrics, this foot can help you apply patch pockets and appliqué, and makes straight edgestitching a breeze!

• You can move the adjustable guide closer to or farther from the left side of the foot to accommodate fabrics of various weights and textures.

• As stitches form, they pass over a metal pin (optional feature) at the center of the foot. This pin adds slack so that stitches are not too taut.

Buttonhole Foot

Whether your project calls for 2 or 12 buttonholes, it's easy to get identical buttonholes with smooth, uniform stitching every time you use a buttonhole foot.

• The top of this foot moves back and forth in a sliding tray attached to the bottom of the foot.

• Markings along one or both sides of the foot indicate buttonhole length.

• Toes at the front or back of foot accommodate cording for corded buttonholes.

• Buttonhole templates in ½", ⅝", ¾", ⅞", and 1" sizes fit into the back of this foot to determine quickly buttonhole length.

Conventional Foot

The conventional, or general purpose, presser foot is most commonly used for everyday sewing.

• The foot's wide opening is proportionate to the width of the machine's zigzag stitch. The width of the opening ranges from ⅛" to ¼" (4 mm to 9 mm), depending on the sewing machine.

• The throat plate used with the conventional foot has an opening of similar size so that the needle can easily enter the bobbin area to form a perfect stitch.

Note From Nancy

The presser feet pictured may not look exactly like the ones in your accessory box because each manufacturer has a different style. To identify your presser feet, check your sewing machine owner's manual, or compare the features listed in this section with your presser feet.

Cording Foot

The cording foot streamlines the process of making piping and couching multiple cords to fabric. It's usually available from your sewing machine dealer.

• The top of the cording foot looks much like the conventional foot with a wide opening for the zigzag stitch.

• The underside has a large, hollowed-out groove to accommodate cording, piping, or decorative trim, allowing the trim to lie flat and feed evenly under the foot.

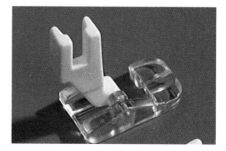

Little Foot™

Accurate piecing is crucial for successful quiltmaking. The Little Foot makes it easy to get that accuracy.

- The right edge of the foot is precisely ¼" (6 mm) from the center needle position, providing an accurate mark for making a ¼" (6 mm) seam allowance.
- The left edge of the foot is precisely ⅛" (3 mm) from the center needle position, providing an accurate mark for making a ⅛" (3 mm) seam allowance.
- Red laser markings ¼" (6 mm) in front of and behind the needle serve as accurate reference points for starting, stopping, and pivoting.

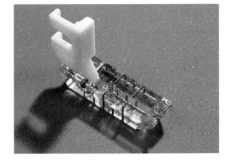

Multicord Foot

If you've ever wrestled with an assortment of decorative threads, trying to keep them aligned as you couch them in place, this presser foot is for you. Use it to guide up to five decorative threads (some feet guide up to nine threads) through the slots and under the foot to create interesting embellishments.

- The multicord foot has five holes in front of the needle opening, three on the top row, and two on the bottom. Feet with nine holes have a third row with four openings.
- Holes accommodate cording or decorative thread.
- Optional: Use a Multiple Cording Guide to keep threads aligned as they feed through the machine. This guide keeps threads separated and controls the flow.

Open Toe or Embroidery Foot

This specialty presser foot lets you see more of the area around the needle when sewing decorative stitches or satin-stitching around appliqué.

- The toe area may be completely open or its center may be clear plastic. This makes it easy to see stitches as they form on fabric.
- The underside has a hollowed or grooved section that allows dense stitching to move smoothly under the foot without bunching under the needle.

Pintuck Foot

A must for creating pintucks, this presser foot has grooves that make it simple to guide and evenly space row after row of pintucks.

- The most distinctive feature of a pintuck foot is the series of grooves on the underside. Depending on the manufacturer, the foot may have five to nine grooves. These grooves provide channels or guides for previous rows of pintucking.
- By combining a pintuck foot with a double needle, you can quickly make straight, uniform pintucks.
- Optional: Insert a cording blade on the machine. This accessory, available for some machines, forces the fabric up into the pintuck foot, making the pintuck more pronounced.

Sequins 'N Ribbons™ Foot

Sew on sequins, ribbons, and even narrow elastic with this unique presser foot.

- An adjustable guide precisely positions the trim in front of the needle.
- Additional accessory guides are available for attaching ⅛" (3 mm) and ⅜" (1 cm) trims and elastics.

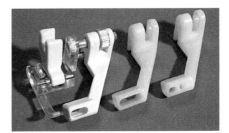

Thread

*For successful sewing, there's more to choosing thread
than just picking the right color.*

Choose thread the same color or one shade darker than your fashion fabric. Thread appears lighter when sewn than it does on the spool. Match thread to the predominant or background color when working with prints, tweeds, or plaids.

If your stitches are not smooth and uniform, check the sewing machine needle for damage, size, and type. The needle should match the thread type, fabric, and sewing technique. The chart that follows includes descriptions of different thread types, their uses, fiber content, and size. Under the size column, the first number (Wt.) indicates the weight of the thread, and the second number (Ply) indicates the number of plies or strands used to make the thread. The larger the weight number, the finer the thread.

Note From Nancy
Always use 3-ply thread for general-purpose sewing. Two-ply thread works well on sergers because serger seams have three or more threads each, which strengthens the seams. I do not recommend using serger thread on your sewing machine.

Thread Type	Description	Uses	Fiber Content	Wt./Ply
All-purpose • Cotton-wrapped polyester core	Polyester core wrapped with fine cotton; less static than 100% polyester, easy to sew with, and withstands high temperatures; can rot or mildew; more durable than 100% cotton, with more stretch and strength	General sewing for most fabrics; avoid on leather, fur, suede, rainwear, and very lightweight fabrics	Cotton and polyester	50/3
• Long-staple polyester	High-quality polyester thread made with long fibers; stronger and more durable than cotton, and more resistant to abrasion and chemicals; may pucker seams and skip stitches in lightweight fabrics	General sewing for most fabrics, including leather, suede, and fur; avoid using on silk and lightweight fabrics	Polyester	50/3
Bobbinfil	Lightweight thread designed specifically for use in the bobbin	Machine embroidery, decorative stitching	100% polyester	70/none
Buttonhole Twist	Thick, heavy thread; sometimes called topstitching thread; less lustrous than silk	Embellishment, topstitching	Polyester or polyester core	40/3

Thread Type	Description	Uses	Fiber Content	Wt./Ply
Cotton	Lightweight thread, double mercerized for sheen and softness	Heirloom sewing, including smocking and embroidery	100% cotton	80/2
Decorative and embellishment threads and yarns	Variety of threads, usually made from cotton, wool, silk, linen, acrylic, or silk-and-wool blend; dry clean or prewash; some fibers may bleed	Surface embellishment, such as couching	Varies	Varies
Embroidery • Cotton	Soft matte finish for a natural appearance	Embroidery, lace-making, quilting	100% cotton	30/2
• Rayon	Brilliant, colorfast thread; available in solid and variegated colors	Decorative stitching, topstitching	100% viscose rayon	40/2, 30/2
Fusible	Adhesive coating on thread melts when pressed with warm iron	Basting; substitute for narrow strips of fusible web	Twisted polyester thread containing heat-activated fusible nylon filament	85/3
Jeans Stitch	Colorfast, durable thread	Topstitching, decorative stitching	Spun polyester	30/3
Lingerie/Bobbin	Extra-fine nylon thread with good stretch; black or white only	Bobbin thread for decorative stitching, machine embroidery, stretch seams	100% nylon with special twist that creates stretch as you sew	70 denier/2
Metallic	Shimmery foil-wrap bonded to thread core; available textured or smooth	Decorative stitching	Foil-wrapped core thread	40/2

Thread Type	Description	Uses	Fiber Content	Wt./Ply
Monofilament (Wonder Thread or Monofil)	Clear, lightweight, soft, single-strand nylon thread; appears invisible when used on the right side of fabric; available clear or smoke-colored	Appliqué, couching, attaching sequins, soft rolled hems, joining lace strips, soft seam finishes, setting pockets, serging	100% nylon filament	.004 size
Serger, All-purpose	Comparable to all-purpose sewing machine thread, except serger thread is 2-ply	Finishing edges, seaming fabrics	Polyester core wrapped with fine cotton or 100% polyester	40/2
Serger, Decorative • Decor 6	Satiny soft thread with extra thickness because plies have minimal twist	Decorative serging, surface embellishment	100% viscose rayon filament	4-ply
• Glamour	Brilliant, glittery durable thread	Decorative serging, surface embellishment	65% viscose rayon, 35% metallic polyester	8-ply
• Pearl Cotton	Very lustrous Egyptian cotton thread	Decorative serging and stitching (size 30/2 is too heavy for stitching on conventional machine)	100% Egyptian cotton, double mercerized for sheen	30/2, 60/2
• Pearl Rayon	Strong, brilliant, colorfast rayon thread; available in solid or variegated colors	Decorative serging, surface embellishment	100% viscose rayon filament	40/2
Silk	Very lustrous	Embellishment, topstitching	100% silk	Varies
Sliver	Thin, flat, ribbonlike polyester film; infused with metal to make it brilliantly reflective	Decorative sewing, serging	Polyester film metalized with aluminum	1/100" thick
Woolly Nylon	Super-stretchy thread used as an edge finish or in seams that require stretch	Serging swimwear, lingerie, baby clothes; especially effective for rolled edges	Texturized (unspun) 100% nylon	DNA

Needles

By choosing the correct needle type and size, you can avoid skipped stitches and fraying thread.

Hand-sewing Needles

• A **crewel needle** is sharp and of medium length, with an elongated eye. It's generally used for embroidery.

• A **double-eyed needle** has blunt tips with eyes on each end that make it useful for weaving threads or trim underneath stitches. Keep the ends of serged seams neat and secure by inserting the thread ends into either of the needle's eyes and threading the needle under the stitches of the seam. Pull the needle through, anchoring the thread ends so that they won't ravel.

Double-eyed needle

Use a double-eyed needle to thread ribbons under decorative serged stitches, to pinweave yarns and ribbons, and to place ribbons in heirloom sewing. Knitters and crocheters appreciate how easily the double-eyed needle secures yarn ends when they change colors or yarn skeins.

• **Sharps** are all-purpose, medium-length needles used for general sewing.

• A **tapestry needle** has a large oval eye and a rounded point. Use it for silk-ribbon embroidery and drawnwork.

• A **weaving needle's** flat shape and bent tip makes it easy to get under warp threads when weaving. This needle's large eye accommodates embellishment yarns, threads, and ribbons.

sharp

tapestry needle

weaving needle

• A **Trolley Needle**™ Thread Controller is not actually a sewing needle, but a sewing guide. Slip a Trolley Needle onto your index finger like a thimble, and use it to ease seams and ruffles under the presser foot or hold ribbon flat while doing silk-ribbon embroidery by machine. You'll also find this a handy tool for positioning sequins and trims while you stitch.

Trolley Needle

Sewing Machine Needles

When choosing a sewing machine needle, you should consider the type and weight of fabric in your project, the type of thread you're using, and the kind of sewing you will be doing.

Some needles have special eyes to accommodate larger threads, others are sturdy enough to stitch heavy fabrics such as denim, and still others are best suited to delicate heirloom sewing on fine fabrics, such as batiste. The Guide to Sewing Machine Needles (on page 18) provides information on needle types, sizes, and appropriate uses.

A sewing machine needle has a shank, a shaft, an eye, and a point. The shank fits into your sewing machine's needle holder, and it has a rounded side and a flat side. The indentation behind the eye is called the scarf. The needle groove is on the same side of the needle as the rounded part of the shaft.

In sewing machine needles, higher numbers identify larger needles, so a size 110 denim needle is larger than a size 90 denim needle. Generally, the larger the needle, the heavier the fabric for which it's appropriate. Use smaller sizes with more delicate fabrics and larger sizes with heavier fabrics.

For double needles, the first size indicates the distance between the two needles, followed by the size of each needle. For example, a 2.0 mm/75 double needle has two size-75 needles that are 2.0 mm apart.

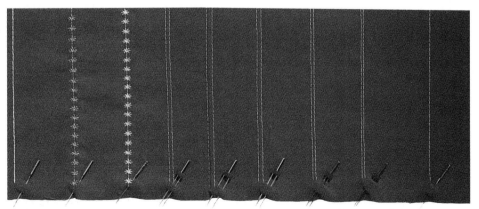

Machine needles and sample stitches shown left to right are: topstitching, metallic, embroidery, double stretch, double 4.0, double 3.0, double 2.0, double 1.6, and all-purpose.

Needle	Size	Description	Uses
Denim/Sharp	90, 100, 110	Very sharp point to ease penetration of dense fabrics	Denim, heavy corduroy, dense wool, canvas, heavy poplin or twill
Leather	80,90	Wedge shape, knife-edge cutting point; not suited for synthetic suede or leather because slit made by needle eventually tears	Real leather or suede; not suitable for synthetic leather or suede
Machine Embroidery	75, 90	Slightly rounded point, long eye, and deep front groove; for use with decorative threads; protects delicate embroidery threads; avoids fraying and breaking	Knits and wovens
Metafil	80	Fine shaft, sharp point, and large, elongated eye; specialized scarf eliminates skipped stitches	Sewing with metallic and other decorative threads
Metallica	80	Large eye for easy threading and to accommodate heavier threads; large groove prevents shredding of threads	Sewing with metallic and other delicate threads
Microtex Sharps	60, 70, 80, 90	Slim, sharp point; very thin shaft for penetrating dense fabric surfaces	Microfiber fabrics such as Ultrasuede; heirloom sewing
Self-threading	90	Slit in side of eye for threading ease; weaker than conventional needles	Simplifies needle threading
Spring Denim/Sharp	100	Sharp point for penetrating dense fabrics; attached spring allows free-form sewing	Free-motion embroidery
Spring Machine Embroidery	75, 90	Same features as machine embroidery needle with an attached spring	Free-motion embroidery using decorative threads
Spring Machine Quilting	75, 90	Same features as machine quilting needle with an attached spring	Free-form quilting
Stretch	75, 90	Medium ballpoint; long, flat shank lets needle work close to bobbin; prevents skipped stitches	Size 75 for sewing lightweight knits, such as tricot, interlock, silk jersey, lycra, and Ultrasuede; size 90 for sewing lycra, Ultrasuede, and synthetic furs with knit backings
Topstitching	80, 90, 100	Extra-large eye; large groove accommodates topstitching thread	Sewing with heavier thread; embroidery with delicate and metallic threads
Universal	60, 70, 80, 90, 100, 110	Slightly rounded point, long needle scarf; all-purpose needle for sewing wovens, knits	Size 60 for silks; size 70 for lightweight fabrics size 80 for medium-weight fabrics; size 90 for medium-weight to heavy fabrics; size 100 for heavy fabrics; size 110 for upholstery fabrics
Wing	100, 120	Wide, wing-shaped blades on each side create holes in fabric that look like entredeux trim	Hemstitch effect for heirloom sewing; best on natural fabrics, such as cotton, linen, silk, organdy
Double	1.6 mm/80 2.0 mm/80 3.0 mm/90 4.0 mm/90 6.0 mm/100 8.0 mm/100	Two universal needles on a crossbar; slightly rounded points	1.6 mm/80 and 2.0 mm/80 for pintucks, delicate heirloom sewing 3.0 mm/90 for hems, pintucks 4.0 mm/90 for decorative hems, surface embellishment 6.0 mm/100 for surface embellishment 8.0 mm/100 for adding texture to fabric
Double Machine Embroidery	2.0 mm/75 3.0 mm/75	Two machine embroidery needles on a crossbar; protects embroidery threads from fraying and breaking	Surface embellishment made with decorative threads
Double Metafil	3.0 mm/80	Two Metafil needles on a crossbar	Double stitching, embellishing with metallic threads
Double Wing	100	One wing needle and one universal needle on a crossbar	Special hemstitch effects and heirloom sewing on natural fabrics, such as cotton, linen, silk, organdy
Double Stretch	2.5 mm/75 4.0 mm/75	Two stretch needles on a crossbar; ballpoint prevents skipped stitches on knits	Pintucking, embroidery on knits, silk jersey, lycra, Ultrasuede
Triple	3.0 mm/80	Three universal needles on a single shaft	Decorative stitching

Interfacings

Interfacing should play a supporting role in almost every garment, adding stability and body.

Fusible Interfacings

The difference between fusible interfacing and fusible web is that fusible interfacing has adhesive on one side only, and fusible web has adhesive on both sides.

For sheer shaping of separates and dresses:
• Fabrics: sheer, lightweight; *batiste, chiffon, dimity, georgette, lawn, voile*
• Brands: Fusible Pellon® #906, Touch O'Gold™

For soft shaping of separates and dresses:
• Fabrics: drapable light- to medium-weight; *challis, jersey, single knits*
• Brands: Pellon® Easy Shaper #114ES, Fusible Pellon® #911FF, Soft 'N Silky™

For crisp shaping of separates and dresses:
• Fabrics: medium-weight; *broadcloth, chambray, cotton blends, gingham, lightweight denim, oxford cloth, poplin*
• Brands: Armo® ShirtShaper, Fusible Pellon® #931TD, Pellon® ShirTailor® #950F, Shape-up® Lightweight, Stacy® Shape

For allover shaping of coats, dresses, jackets, and suits:
• Fabrics: medium- to heavyweight; *corduroy, denim, flannel, linen, poplin, tweed, wool, wool blends*
• Brands: Armo® Fusi-Form™ Lightweights, SuitMaker™, Pellon® Sof-Shape® #880F, SofBrush™, SofTouch™

For crisp shaping of coats, dresses, jackets, and suits:
• Fabrics: medium- to heavyweight; *gabardine, mohair, synthetic leather, synthetic suede*
• Brands: Armo® Form-Flex™

Nonwoven, Armo® Fusi-Form™ Suitweight, Pellon® Pel-Aire® #881, Whisper Weft™

For knits only:
• Fabrics: *cotton/blended knits, double knits, jersey, lightweight velour, single knits, sweatshirt fleece, terry*
• Brands: Knit fuze®, Pellon® Stretch-Ease #921, Quick Knit™, SofKnit®, Stacy® Easy-Knit® #130EK

For crafts:
• Fabrics: all
• Brands: Pellon® Craft-Bond®

Fusible Webs

Woven or nonwoven fusible web has adhesive on both sides, and may have paper covering one side. You can also buy fusible thread and liquid fusible web, which acts like heat-activated fabric glue.

Paper-backed, no-sew fusible web
• Use for crafts, home-decorating projects; light- to medium-weight fabrics; dense web gums needle if stitched through
• Brands: HeatnBond® UltraHold, Pellon® Heavy Duty, Wonder-Under®

Paper-backed fusible web
• Use for appliqués, hems; light-, medium-, heavyweight fabrics; transfer designs onto paper backing, which acts as built-in pressing sheet; OK to sew through
• Brands: Aleene's Original Fusible Web™, Aleene's Ultra Hold Fusible Web™, HeatnBond® Lite, Pellon® Wonder-Under® Fusing Web, Stitch Witchery® Plus with Grid

Fusible web
• Use for appliqués, hems; light-, medium-, heavyweight fabrics
• Brands: Fine Fuse, Stitch Witchery®

Liquid fusible web
• Use for hems, appliqués, emblems, ribbons, other trims; reposition ribbons, appliqués before you heat-set liquid fusible; bottle's applicator tip makes it easy to control amount and placement
• Brands: Aleene's Liquid Fusible Web™, Liqui Fuse™ Liquid Fusible Web™

Fusible thread
• Use for basting zippers, hems; heat and steam from iron cause thread to fuse fabrics together
• Brands: Stitch 'n Fuse®, ThreadFuse™

Stabilizers

Stabilizers add body to fabric and prevent puckering, pulling, or tearing of stitches.

Iron-on stabilizer
• Use for appliqué, machine embroidery, especially on stretchy, delicate fabrics; iron on, then tear away
• Brands: Totally Stable

Liquid stabilizer
• Use for appliqué, machine embroidery; apply to fabric and let dry; wash away after stitching
• Brands: Perfect Sew

Tear-away stabilizer
• Use for appliqué, machine embroidery
• Brands: Pellon® Stitch-N-Tear®, Tear Easy Stabilizer®

Water-soluble stabilizer
• Use for machine embroidery on knit or woven fabrics; apply to right or wrong side of fabric; press away using a wet press cloth, or place project under water
• Brands: Avalon Soluble Stabilizer, Wash-Away Plastic Stabilizer

Stitch thread scraps and fabric bits into a Scribble Collage *(left and page 29)*. Zigzag over colorful thread in a simple design and you've added Basic Couching *(right and page 22)* to a vest. ▶

Using nothing more than a sewing machine or serger and thread, you can embroider, quilt, and even create custom fabric.

Versatile Threads

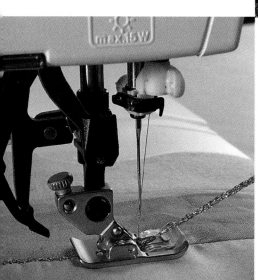

Easy hints, such as inserting decorative yarn through the top of an embroidery foot *(left and page 22)*, make these embellishments a snap. Fused braid and satin-stitched leaf ribs create this Pseudo Battenberg vest *(right and page 36)*. ▶

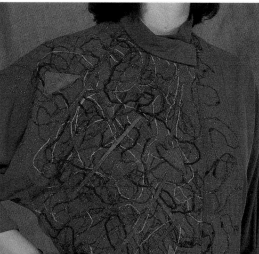

Place stabilizer on top of the area you plan to embellish and use metallic thread in a double needle to stitch the Windowpane Collage blouse *(left and page 27)*.

Top-Thread Sashiko Dress,
page 32

Couching

Zigzagging over thread, yarns, ribbon, decorative serger thread, or cording is a novel yet simple way to add highlights to fabric.

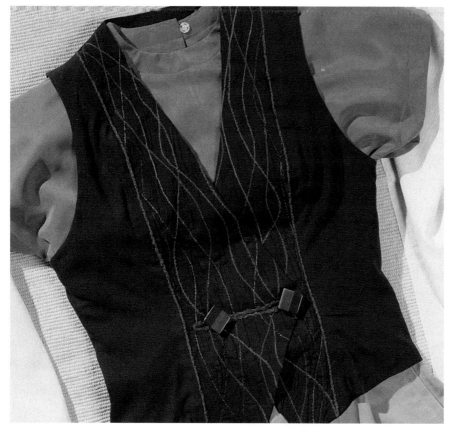

Couching techniques range from single-yarn to multiple-yarn or thread embellishments.

Gather Basic Supplies

Listed are general supplies for couching. Additional notions streamline specialized couching techniques; you'll find those listed with the specific technique.

❑ Monofilament thread
❑ Thread that matches fabric
❑ Decorative yarn
❑ Embroidery foot
❑ Metafil needle
❑ Iron-on stabilizer

Select Fabric

Choose a solid-colored fashion fabric to embellish that coordinates with the decorative yarns. See your pattern for fabric amount.

Get Ready

✔ Replace the conventional foot with an embroidery foot.
✔ Insert a metafil needle.
✔ Thread the top of the machine with monofilament thread.
✔ Use thread matched to the fabric in the bobbin.
✔ Set the machine for a medium-width and medium-length zigzag stitch.

Create Basic Couching

1. Use your pattern to cut out the fabric.
2. Back the fabric pieces with an iron-on stabilizer.
3. Insert decorative yarn through the top zigzag opening in the front of the embroidery foot.

Yarn placement in an embroidery foot

Note from Nancy

Inserting decorative yarn through the opening in the foot gives you greater control over the yarn when stitching a meandering pattern.
To follow a specific design, simply place the yarn on the fabric and lower the presser foot over the yarn for easiest control.

4. Zigzag or couch over the decorative yarns, stitching in a meandering pattern. The zig should fall on one side of the yarn, and the zag on the other side.
5. Remove the stabilizer from the wrong side of the fabric.

Highlighted Couching

Note from Nancy

Another option is to follow a design when you couch over yarns. To make this vest, I marked the chevron design on the fabric with chalk before couching over yarns.

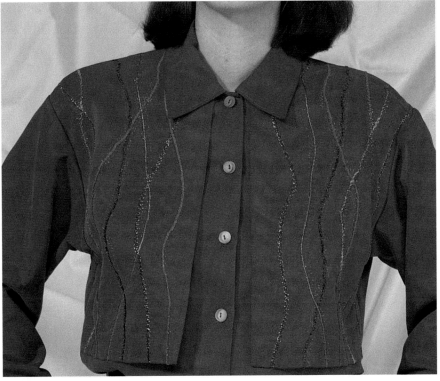

Gather Supplies

❑ Metallic or metallic ribbonlike thread

❑ Metallic needle

Get Ready

✔ Insert a metallic needle in your machine.

✔ Thread the top of your sewing machine with the metallic or metallic ribbonlike thread.

Note from Nancy

For best results, metallic ribbonlike thread should unwind from the side of the spool, so you should place the spool in a vertical position. If your machine holds the spool in a horizontal position, use a Horizontal Spool Feeder to change the spool to a vertical position.

✔ Loosen the top tension by two notches or positions.

✔ Use thread matched to the fabric in the bobbin.

✔ Choose an airy, decorative stitch or a common utility stitch, such as blindhem, feather, or scribble stitch.

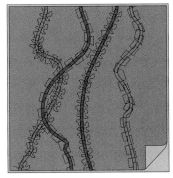

Decorative stitches used for couching

Create Highlighted Couching

Follow the instructions for Basic Couching. The elements of metallic threads and decorative stitches add interest to basic couching.

23

Quick-Twist Couching

Photo A: Insert decorative threads through thread lasso on bobbin.

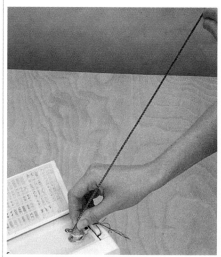

Photo B: Hold thread vertically and pinch together at bobbin.

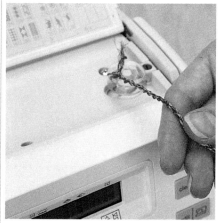

Photo C: Strands automatically twist into decorative cording.

Quick-Twisting Cording

Add variety and texture to fabric by couching over cording created by twisting together decorative threads.

Gather Supplies

❑ Cording foot
❑ Empty bobbin
❑ Decorative threads or yarns:
   Decorative serger thread
   Metallic threads
   Decorative yarns
❑ Monofilament or metallic thread for needle
❑ Thread for bobbin that matches the fabric

Get Ready

✔ Set up the sewing machine as detailed on page 22 in Get Ready for Basic Couching, except replace the embroidery foot with a cording foot.

Create Quick-Twist Couching

1. Quick-twist several strands of decorative thread to create cording.

• Cut several lengths of decorative thread or yarns at least four times the length needed for the finished cording.

• Insert a 3" to 4" (7.5 cm to 10 cm) piece of strong thread through the opening in a bobbin and tie the thread ends to form a lasso. Insert the decorative threads through the lasso; meet thread cut ends (*Photo A*). The doubled thread should be at least twice the length needed for the finished cording.

• Attach the bobbin to the sewing machine as if you were winding a bobbin. If necessary, disengage the fly wheel.

• Hold the cut ends of the threads vertically with one hand; lightly pinch the threads together at the bobbin (*Photo B*).

Fringed Couching

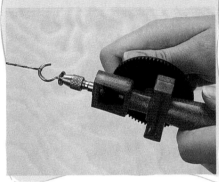

• Run the sewing machine as if winding the bobbin. The threads will twist together.

• When the threads are tightly twisted, meet the cut ends to the lasso and grasp the four strands together. Let go of the remaining thread end. The four strands will automatically twist together, creating thread that resembles heavy cording *(Photo C).*

• Clip the thread at the lasso. Remove the bobbin and reset the machine for stitching.

2. Couch over the quick-twist cording, using a zigzag stitch as described in Basic Couching.

1. Quick-twist two or more strands of thread together.

2. Couch over the threads as previously described.

3. Create fringed sections:

• Stop stitching with the needle down in the fabric *(Diagram A).*

• If your machine has a "needle up/down" feature, set the sewing machine so that the needle stops in the down position.

• Raise the presser foot. Wrap the quick-twist cording around the back of the needle, allowing a loop to form.

• Bring the quick twist to the front of the needle. Lower the presser foot and continue stitching, securing the loop to the fabric.

• Repeat, creating additional loops.

• After adding as many loops as desired, cut the loops, and the quick-twist cording will fringe *(Diagram B).*

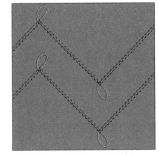

Diagram A: Stop stitching with needle down.

Diagram B: Cut loops to create fringe.

Controlled Couching

Gather Supplies

❏ Water-soluble stabilizer
❏ Sequins 'N Ribbon™ Foot or cording foot
❏ Ribbon or sequins by the yard

Get Ready

✔ Replace the conventional foot with a ribbon or cording foot.
✔ Set up the sewing machine as for Basic Couching.
✔ Thread ribbon or sequins through the ribbon foot's accessory guide or under the opening of the cording foot.

Sequins 'N Ribbon foot

Note from Nancy

Before threading the sequins through the opening of the foot, brush the sequin strand with your finger to determine the smooth (napped) direction. Insert the strand in the guide so that you stitch in the direction of the nap.

Create Controlled Couching

1. Draw a design on a piece of water-soluble stabilizer.
2. Place the stabilizer over the right side of the fabric (*Diagram A*).

Carefully flip the fabric over to the wrong side. Press, using a steam iron, to fuse stabilizer to fabric. This fusing isn't permanent, but the stabilizer adheres long enough to prevent the fabric from shifting during stitching.
3. Couch over the ribbon or sequins. Zigzag, following the traced design on the stabilizer.
• If possible, adjust the machine so that the needle stops in the down position, making it easier to turn the fabric.
• Shorten the stitch length and stitch slower when couching in curved areas.
4. Carefully tear away large sections of the water-soluble stabilizer.
5. Remove the stabilizer from the interior of the design by spritzing with water. If the fabric or trim is not washable, press away the remaining stabilizer as follows.
• Cover design with a damp press cloth.
• Press, and the stabilizer will adhere to or be absorbed onto the press cloth (*Diagram B*).

• Repeat this process as necessary, rinsing out the press cloth between pressings.

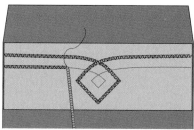

Diagram A: Place stabilizer over right side of fabric.

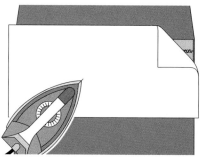

Diagram B: Remove stabilizer using a damp press cloth.

Thread Collages

Here is a thread lover's version of a collage!

Simply scatter a selection of threads and appliqué shapes on top of your fabric palette. Add stitching and you've made a one-of-a-kind embellishment.

Gather Supplies

❑ Threads for collage (choose your favorites):
   Ribbon Floss
   Embroidery threads
   Decorative serger threads
   Decorative yarns
❑ Metallic or machine embroidery thread for needle
❑ Thread that matches fabric for bobbin
❑ Paper-backed fusible web
❑ Water-soluble stabilizer
❑ 3.0 or 4.0 double needle
❑ Quilting bar

Select Fabric

Choose fashion fabric for the garment. See your pattern for amount.

Choose coordinating, tightly woven or nonraveling fabric scraps for appliqué. The garment shown features Ultrasuede appliqués.

Get Ready

✔ Insert the double needle in your machine.
✔ Thread two spools of metallic or machine embroidery thread on the top of the machine, threading them as one until they reach the needle. Then separate the threads and insert each through one needle.
✔ Use thread matched to the fashion fabric in the bobbin.
✔ Attach a quilting bar to the presser foot, setting the bar ¾" to 1" (2 cm to 2.5 cm) from the needle.

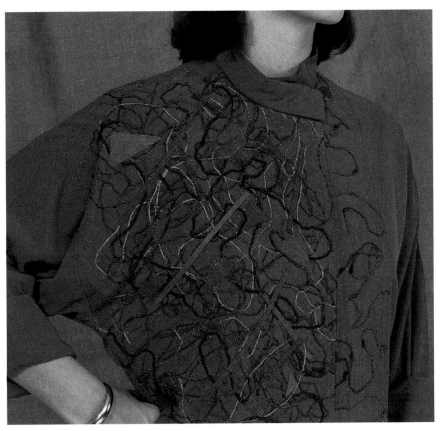

Note from Nancy
If you have only one spool of the color you're using, wind two bobbins. Use one as the bobbin thread as usual; use the other as the second thread spool on top of the machine.

Quilting bar attached to presser foot

Create a Windowpane Collage

1. Unwind the collage threads and place them on the fabric in a random arrangement, creating a pleasing abstract design *(Diagram A on page 28)*. Extend the threads to the seam lines of the garment section; you don't have to extend the threads into seam allowances.

Note from Nancy
Bobbins from previous projects are a great source of thread for these collages. When you unwind the tightly coiled thread, it has graceful curls and swirls.

2. Add geometric appliqués.

• Back coordinating fabric scraps with paper-backed fusible web.

• Cut the fabric into desired shapes.

• Place these appliqués within the thread arrangement.

• Press to fuse the appliqués in place *(Diagram B)*.

3. Place a layer of water-soluble stabilizer on top of the fabric. Pin securely in place *(Diagram C)*.

> *Note from Nancy*
> *Stabilizers are traditionally placed under fabric for decorative stitching. However, by placing stabilizer on top of the collage, you hold the thread in position during stitching and also stabilize the area. The stabilizer also offers a convenient surface to mark the position for the first line of stitching.*

4. Stitch a windowpane design over the positioned threads and fabrics.

• Mark one line on the water-soluble stabilizer. This line may be vertical, horizontal, or on the bias.

• Stitch along the marked line *(Diagram D)*.

• Align the edge of the quilting bar with the first row of stitching. Stitch additional rows parallel to the first row, spaced equally apart, guiding the quilting bar along the previously sewn row *(Diagram E)*.

• Repeat until you have stitched the entire piece.

• Mark one cross row at a 90° angle to the first rows and stitch along that row.

• Stitch additional cross rows until you have stitched the entire piece into a windowpane effect, again using the quilting bar as a guide *(Diagram F)*.

5. Remove the water-soluble stabilizer.

Stitching a Windowpane Collage

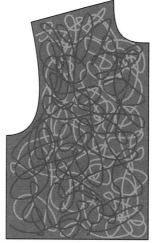

Diagram A: Place collage threads in a pleasing design.

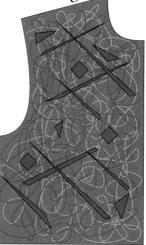

Diagram B: Fuse geometric appliqués in place.

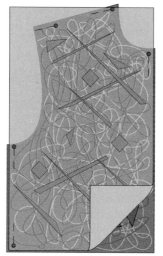

Diagram C: Pin stabilizer on top of collage.

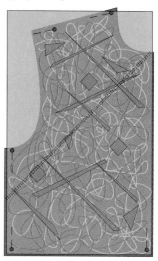

Diagram D: Mark and stitch first line.

Diagram E: Stitch rows parallel to first stitching.

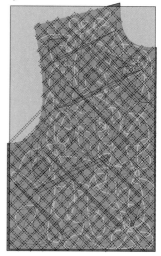

Diagram F: Complete windowpane grid of stitches.

Scribble Collage

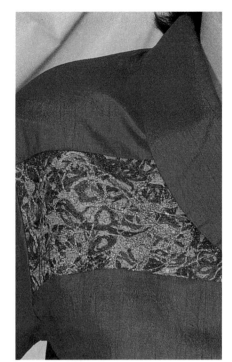

A thread collage takes on a different look when you substitute a sheer backing for the fashion fabric and replace the double-needle stitching with a scribble stitch. This collage application can give your project a dramatic look.

Gather Supplies

❑ Threads for collage (choose your favorites):
    Ribbon Floss
    Embroidery threads
    Decorative serger threads
    Decorative yarns
❑ Machine embroidery thread for needle
❑ Thread that matches fabric for bobbin
❑ Water-soluble stabilizer
❑ Machine embroidery needle and thread

Select Fabric

Select a lightweight fabric, such as organza or batiste, as the background fabric for the collage.

Get Ready

✔ Set the machine for a programmed scribble stitch (available on some sewing machines). A scribble stitch resembles a random stitch pattern. If your machine doesn't have this feature, select a wide zigzag or multiple-step zigzag stitch.
✔ Use the conventional presser foot.
✔ Insert a machine embroidery needle.
✔ Thread the machine with embroidery thread in the needle.
✔ Use thread matched to the fabric in the bobbin.

Create Scribble Collage

1. Create the collage over the lightweight fabric; cover it with water-soluble stabilizer.
2. Stitch over the thread collage with a scribble stitch or zigzag stitch *(Diagram)*.
3. Remove the water-soluble stabilizer.

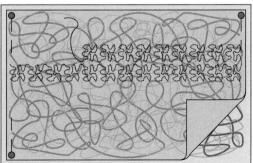

Diagram: Sew over thread collage using a scribble stitch or a random stitch pattern.

Create a Plaid

Stitching on the diagonal is a worry-free way to match plaids.
This creative embellishment takes time, but the results are well worth the effort!

Gather Supplies

❑ Iron-on stabilizer
❑ Quilting ruler
❑ Chalk
❑ Embroidery or metallic thread for needle
❑ Thread that matches fabric for bobbin
❑ Machine embroidery needle or metallic needle
❑ Embroidery or open toe foot

Select Fabric

Choose a solid-colored fabric. See your pattern for amount.

Get Ready

✔ Insert a machine embroidery needle or a metallic needle, depending upon which thread is used.

✔ Thread the top of the machine with decorative thread. Experiment with various threads.
✔ Use thread that matches the fabric in the bobbin.
✔ Loosen the top tension by two numbers or notches (for example, from 5 to 3).
✔ Replace the conventional presser foot with an embroidery or open toe foot.
✔ Set the machine for a decorative stitch.

Note from Nancy
Totally Stable is a paperlike stabilizer with a waxy coating on the wrong side. Ironing temporarily adheres the stabilizer to the fabric, yet Totally Stable tears away easily.

Create a Plaid

1. Press iron-on stabilizer to the wrong side of the fabric (*Diagram A*). Stabilizer prevents the fabric from shifting or moving during decorative stitching.
2. Grid the fabric.
• Press or use chalk to mark the lengthwise grain line on the right side of the fabric.

Note from Nancy
Use white chalk on dark fabric and blue or yellow chalk on light-colored fabric. Always test chalk marks on a scrap of fabric before marking your project to be sure they show up and that they will come out of the fabric when you finish stitching.

• Align the 45° angle on a quilting ruler with the lengthwise mark. Use chalk to mark the diagonal line (*Diagram B*). Retrace the line if needed to provide a heavy coating of chalk.
• Mark additional lines parallel to the first line, spaced 4½" (11.5 cm) apart, until you mark the entire fabric (*Diagram C*).
• Mark another set of lines at right angles to the first lines, again spaced 4½" (11.5 cm) apart. Be certain all lines have a heavy concentration of chalk.
• Stack the corresponding fabrics pieces, right sides together. Rub or hand-press the fabric until the chalk transfers to the second piece, creating a perfect mirror image (*Diagram D*).

Creating Plaid

Diagram A: Fuse stabilizer to wrong side of fabric.

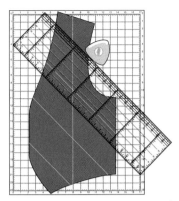

Diagram B: Use a quilting ruler and chalk to mark diagonal lines.

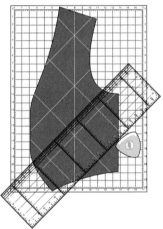

Diagram C: Continue marking until entire fabric is gridded.

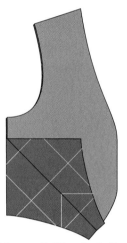

Diagram D: Transfer chalk pattern to unmarked garment piece.

Diagram E: Stitch design, using thread colors and stitches as determined from test strips.

Note from Nancy
If your decorative plaid design goes on only one piece of fabric, you don't need a heavy concentration of chalk to mark the decorative stitching lines.

• Rechalk lines on the fabric if necessary.

3. Plan the design by testing stitching strips.

• Cut 1" (2.5 cm) strips of the fashion fabric.

• Fuse stabilizer to the strips.

• Sew different decorative stitches on each strip. Stitches with geometric designs are especially suited for the plaid. Vary thread colors as you stitch the test strips.

• Arrange and rearrange the strips of the various colors and stitches until the design pleases you. Do this by placing the strips on the diagonal grid to determine the number and arrangement of stitches for the finished plaid. (It's like arranging puzzle pieces.)

4. Once you decide on the design, stitch the design on the fabric, using the threads and stitches from your puzzle arrangement *(Diagram E).*

Note from Nancy
Don't be in a hurry to do this stitching. Creating the plaid is easy, but it is also time consuming. Take your time, and enjoy!

5. Remove the stabilizer when you have finished stitching.

6. Complete your garment or project following your pattern directions.

Sashiko

Create this Japanese hand embellishment entirely by machine.

When you machine-stitch Sashiko from the right side of fabric, the thread highlights are less pronounced than in traditional, hand-stitched Sashiko, because heavyweight thread cannot easily pass through a sewing machine needle. My variation lets you choose more dramatic threads, and it is the easiest way to machine-stitch Sashiko embellishments.

Gather Supplies

❑ Metallic or machine embroidery thread (two spools) for needle
❑ Thread that matches fabric for bobbin
❑ Water-soluble stabilizer
❑ Machine embroidery or metallic needle

Select Fabric

Choose a dark solid-colored fabric. (Denim is traditional.) Check your pattern for amount.

Get Ready

✔ Insert a metallic or machine embroidery needle that corresponds with the top thread.
✔ Use two strands of thread on top of the machine, threading them through the machine as if they were a single strand. I created the embellishment on the black evening dress using two spools of metallic thread.
✔ Use thread that matches the fabric in the bobbin.
✔ Loosen the top tension by one or two notches to keep the bobbin thread on the underside of the fabric. For example, adjust the tension from 5 to 3.
✔ Set the machine for a straightstitch.

Create Top-Thread Sashiko

1. Trace the design on a section of water-soluble stabilizer; pin or press the stabilizer to the right side of the fabric *(Diagram)*. The pattern I used appears on page 135.
2. Stitch the design.
• Practice stitching on a scrap to determine an appropriate stitch length.

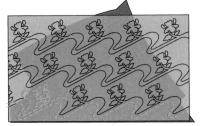

Diagram: Trace design on stabilizer and pin or press to right side of fabric.

Note from Nancy
Traditional Sashiko features a long running stitch. With the sewing machine, I use a medium-length stitch, because a longer stitch makes it more difficult to maneuver curves. As you stitch, sew at a slow, constant speed and turn the fabric with both hands, like turning a steering wheel. Practice on a scrap so that you get the feel of the stitching.

• Stitch continuously to complete the design. Adjust the machine to stop with the needle in the down position (if possible) to simplify the sewing process.

3. Remove the water-soluble stabilizer.

• Cut or tear away as much of the stabilizer as possible.

• To remove the remaining stabilizer and any residue from fabric that is washable, spritz the stabilizer with water.

• If the fabric isn't washable, place a very damp (almost wet) cloth over the stabilizer and press. The stabilizer adheres to and is absorbed into the press cloth. If necessary, rinse the press cloth and repeat until you remove all the stabilizer.

Bobbin-Work Sashiko

Gather Supplies

❑ All-purpose thread for the needle that matches the decorative bobbin thread

❑ Heavyweight thread, such as top-stitching thread, buttonhole twist, or jeans thread, for the bobbin

❑ Water-soluble stabilizer

❑ Topstitching needle, size 90 or 100

Select Fabric

Choose a dark solid-colored fabric. (Denim is traditional.) Check your pattern for amount.

Get Ready

✔ Insert the topstitching needle in your machine.

✔ Thread the top of the machine with all-purpose thread.

✔ Wind the bobbin with heavy-weight thread.

✔ Set machine for a straightstitch with a medium stitch length.

✔ Tighten the top tension by one or two notches so that the top thread stays on the surface of the fabric. For example, adjust the tension from 5 to 7.

Create Bobbin-Work Sashiko

1. Trace the Sashiko design onto a section of water-soluble stabilizer. Place the stabilizer on the wrong

side of the fabric; pin in place *(Diagram).*

2. Stitch the Sashiko design from the wrong side.

• Practice stitching on a scrap to determine an appropriate stitch length.

• Stitch continuously to complete the design, sewing at a slow, constant speed to make maneuvering curves easier. Adjust the machine to stop with the needle in the down position (if possible) to simplify the sewing process.

3. Remove the stabilizer from the wrong side of the fabric after stitching is completed. Pull threads to the wrong side; tie and clip threads.

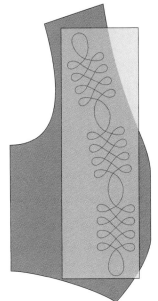

Diagram: Pin stabilizer with design to wrong side of fabric.

Rambling Pintucks with Trapunto

Create a dramatic effect by using pintucks to frame trapunto, a raised Italian quilting design.

Gather Supplies

- ❑ 3.0 and 4.0 double needles
- ❑ Pintuck foot
- ❑ Cording foot
- ❑ Batting or fiberfill
- ❑ Embroidery floss
- ❑ Serger looper threader
- ❑ Machine embroidery thread (two spools) for needle
- ❑ Thread that matches fabric for bobbin
- ❑ Thread to use as cording for pintucks such as pearl cotton or pearl rayon, serger thread, embroidery floss, or ⅛" (3 mm) cable cord

Select Fabrics

Choose a lightweight, drapable fabric. Check your pattern for amount.

Get Ready

- ✔ Insert the double needle in your machine.
- ✔ Thread two spools of machine embroidery thread on top of the machine, threading them as one until they reach the needle. Then separate the threads and insert each through its respective needle.
- ✔ Use thread matched to the fashion fabric in the bobbin.
- ✔ Replace the conventional foot with a pintuck foot.

Create Rambling Pintucks with Trapunto

1. Add the embellishment before cutting out the garment. Cut the fabric 3" to 4" (7.5 cm to 10 cm) wider than the pattern piece to allow for the width and length that the embellishment will take up.

2. Add dimension with trapunto.

• Determine approximately where you want to place the trapunto and mark with pins *(Diagram A)*.

• Cut a small section of quilt batting or fiberfill the size and shape of the trapunto design.

> *Note from Nancy*
> *Try out various shapes before choosing a specific trapunto design. Small abstract or geometric shapes often are more attractive than large designs. In this instance, "less is best" is good advice.*

• Place the batting on the wrong side of the fabric behind the pin-marked areas.

• Hand-baste around outer edges of the batting to create stitching guides *(Diagram B)*.

3. Use thread or cording to add dimension to the pintucks. Place lightweight cording, such as floss, serger thread, pearl cotton, or pearl rayon, in your lap. Insert the cording through the opening in the sewing machine throat plate, threading the cording from the underside and drawing the cord through to the back of the machine. As you stitch, the cording will automatically be included on the underside of the fabric, which will help raise the pintuck.

> *Note from Nancy*
> *A serger looper threader makes this job easier. Insert the serger looper threader through the hole in the throat plate from the top, and pull the thread up from the bobbin area.*

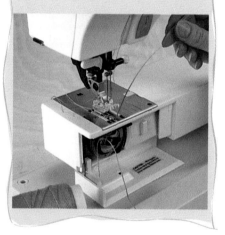

4. Begin stitching pintucks.

• Stitch the first row, gently turning the fabric to create a curved, rambling pattern. At the trapunto areas, sew next to the basting stitch to catch the edge of the batting and secure it in place *(Diagram C)*.

• Stitch another row, placing the first pintuck row in one of the pintuck foot's outer grooves.

• Stitch additional rows, generally sewing parallel to the first row. You can vary the distance between pintuck rows by placing previously stitched rows at different positions in the grooved foot.

5. Stitch the second side of the rambling pattern, making numerous rows of pintucks, following the same guidelines as for the first section *(Diagram D)*.

Note from Nancy

Showcase your creativity by adding an exaggerated pintuck. Attach a piping foot and the wider 4.0 double needle. Place cable cord under the fabric and stitch over the cording (Diagram E). This exaggerated pintuck has greater dimension, comparable to the raised effect of the trapunto. In the purple jacket shown on page 34, I stitched the exaggerated pintucks on the outside of the design.

6. Add hand-stitched embellishments.
• Hand-stitch along the side of the pintucks, using heavier threads, such as silk floss or embroidery thread.
• Add French knots or other embroidery stitching as desired *(Diagram F)*.
7. Remove basting threads along the trapunto edges.
8. Back the fabric with a facing or lining.

Framing Trapunto with Pintucks

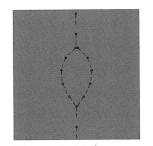

Diagram A: Mark trapunto design with pins.

Diagram B: Hand-baste to make stitching guides.

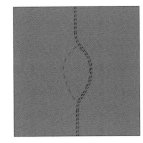

Diagram C: Sew through batting next to basting.

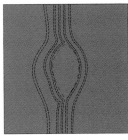

Diagram D: Add pintucks to opposite side of trapunto.

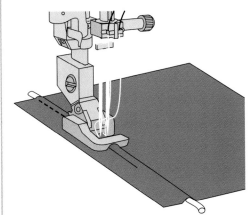

Diagram E: Exaggerate pintucks by stitching over cording.

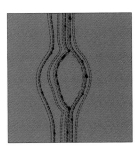

Diagram F: Add hand-embroidery stitches as desired.

Pseudo Battenberg

Duplicate any Battenberg design with thread, braid, and savvy zigzag stitching.

Gather Supplies

❑ Lightweight fusible interfacing
❑ Transfer pen and paper or dress-maker's tracing paper
❑ Embroidery needle or metallic needle
❑ Metallic or machine embroidery thread that matches or coordinates with braid for needle
❑ Lingerie/bobbin thread for bobbin
❑ Embroidery foot
❑ Liquid fusible web
❑ 4 mm-wide braid
❑ Press cloth

Select Fabrics

Choose a base color. Check your pattern for amount.

Get Ready

✔ Insert a needle that coordinates with the thread (metallic or machine embroidery).

✔ Thread the top of the machine with machine embroidery or metallic thread.
✔ Use a lightweight thread, such as lingerie/bobbin thread, in the bobbin.
✔ Replace the conventional presser foot with an embroidery foot. Loosen the top tension by two numbers or notches.
✔ Adjust the machine for a narrow zigzag. As a starting point, set the stitch width at 1 and the stitch length at .5. Test stitching on a scrap before stitching on the actual project.

Create Pseudo Battenberg

1. Fuse lightweight interfacing to the wrong side of the fabric for added support.
2. Transfer the design to the fabric in one of the following ways. The design

I used appears on page 138.
• Trace the design on transfer paper using a transfer pen. Place the transfer paper face down on the fabric. Rub, pressing with your thumbnail or a tool like the Little Wooden Iron (Diagram A).

> ### Note from Nancy
> I sometimes use the Fabric Pattern Transfer Kit to transfer designs to fabric. The kit includes two reusable Transfer Rice Paper sheets and a double-sided fabric transfer pen (the purple tip marks the fabric and the white tip erases the mark). Consider using this timesaving notion when transferring silk-ribbon embroidery patterns to fabric. Learn how to stitch silk-ribbon embroidery by machine in Chapter 6.

• Trace the design onto tissue paper. Place dressmaker's tracing paper on top of the fabric, carbon side down, with the tissue tracing on top. Use a blunt pencil or fingernail to trace over the image (Diagram B).

> ### Note from Nancy
> When you transfer the design, remember that you get the reverse, or mirror image, of the traced design. If you want the design to appear exactly like the original, flip the design so that you trace a mirror image. As always, test this or any transfer method on a fabric scrap before using it on the actual project.

3. Satin-stitch the inside ribs or veins of the design.

• Stitch over one of the lines in the design. Raise the presser foot and advance the fabric to the next line without cutting the threads.

• After stitching all inside lines of one section, clip the top thread tails *(Diagram C).*

4. Apply a fine line of liquid fusible web along the outer lines of the transferred design. Let dry *(Diagram D).*

Note from Nancy
Liqui Fuse Liquid Fusible Web is an ideal product to hold braid temporarily. Apply this gluelike liquid in a fine line, making it easier to shape braid into intricate designs.

5. Place the braid over the liquid fusible web and cut the braid to size.

• Work on a padded pressing surface.

• Tuck the cut ends of the braid under a continuous strip of the braid.

• Shape the braid to conform to the design. *(Diagram E).* If necessary, fold the braid back on itself to form tight angles or corners.

• Pin the braid to the fabric, using enough pins to hold the shape.

6. To position the braid temporarily, cover it with a press cloth and press 40 to 50 seconds, following manufacturers instructions. Remove pins.

7. Permanently stitch the braid to the fabric.

• Adjust machine for a zigzag slightly narrower than the braid.

• Zigzag down the center of the braid *(Diagram F).*

Creating Pseudo Battenberg Designs

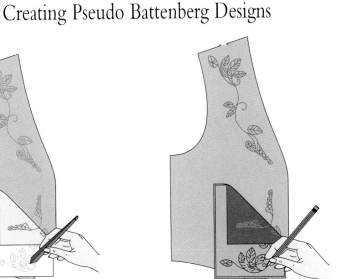

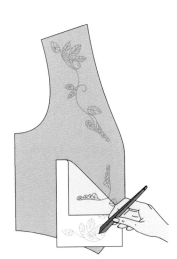

Diagram A: Use transfer paper to mark design.

Diagram B: Use tissue and tracing paper to transfer design.

Diagram C: Satin-stitch inside details; clip thread tails.

Diagram D: Apply liquid fusible web to outer lines of design.

Diagram E: Place braid over fusible web, shaping to fit design.

Diagram F: Stitch down center of braid.

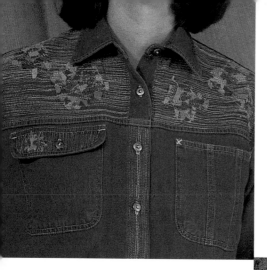

◀ Confetti appliqué *(left and page 47)* adds a casual look that's easy to make and fun to wear. Small shapes of Ultrasuede make a striking and easy accent for a jacket *(right and page 56).* ▶

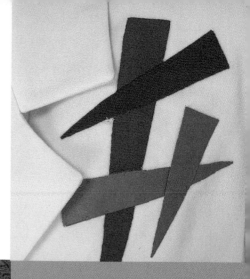

Dress up even simple appliqués with metallic threads, or make the stitching almost invisible by using monofilament nylon thread.

Uncommon Appliqué

◀ Decorative buttons and buttonholes impart a folk-art look to fringed buttonhole appliqués *(left and page 52).* Ultrasuede on a pocket finishes off a simple outfit, such as this chambray shirt *(right and page 57).* ▶

◀ Liquid fabric solvent is the secret to quick and easy cutwork appliqué *(left and page 54).*

Framed-Stitch Appliqué,
page 58

Invisibly Stitched Appliqués

Create a machine-sewn embellishment that looks like you stitched it by hand.

This charming invisibly stitched option features the ever-popular Sunbonnet Sue design. Look for additional design choices in appliqué and quilting books.

Gather Supplies

❑ Conventional sewing machine foot
❑ Thread that matches the fabric for needle and bobbin
❑ Metafil needle
❑ Lightweight fusible interfacing
❑ Bamboo Pointer & Creaser
❑ Liquid fusible web
❑ Press cloth
❑ Embroidery or open toe foot
❑ Monofilament nylon thread

Select Fabrics

Choose fashion fabric. See your pattern for amount.

Choose cotton or cotton blend coordinating fabric scraps for appliqués.

Get Ready

✔ Attach the conventional foot (you will replace it with an embroidery or open toe foot later).
✔ Thread the needle and bobbin with all-purpose thread to match the fashion fabric.
✔ Insert a metafil needle.
✔ Set the machine for a straightstitch with a short length, approximately 15 stitches per inch.

Create Invisibly Stitched Appliqués

1. Trace the elements of the appliqué design to the nonfusible side of the interfacing, leaving ½" (1.3 cm) of

space between the designs. (See page 138 for our Sunbonnet Sue appliqué pattern.) Cut out pieces, allowing approximately ¼" (6 mm) seam allowances *(Diagram A)*.

2. Cut out the fabrics for the appliqués, approximately the same size as the interfacing pieces.

3. Meet the right side of the fabric to the nonfusible side of the interfacing. You may want to redraw the tracing on the fusible side of the interfacing. Stitch around the traced design with a short stitch length *(Diagram B)*.

Note from Nancy
A short stitch length makes it easier to stitch curves on small pieces. The shorter stitches reinforce the seam and give you greater accuracy when stitching a curve.

4. Trim the seam allowance to approximately ⅛" (3 mm).

5. Cut a slit in the center of the interfacing, taking care not to cut through the appliqué fabric *(Diagram C)*. Turn the appliqué right side out.

Invisibly Stitched Appliqué

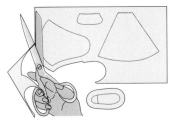

Diagram A: Cut out pattern, adding ¼" seam allowances.

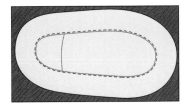

Diagram B: Stitch around traced design.

Diagram C: Slit interfacing; turn right side out.

Diagram D: Apply liquid fusible web to edges.

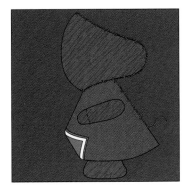

Diagram E: Stitch using monofilament thread.

6. Use a tool with a rounded point to obtain crisp edges on the appliqué. Roll the seam to the edge of the appliqué between your fingers, and press with the tip of the iron. The fusible interfacing adheres the two layers, giving sharp, crisp edges.

> ### Note from Nancy
> A Bamboo Pointer & Creaser is an ideal notion to use when turning appliqué pieces right side out. The rounded point easily brings the seam to the appliqué edge without making a hole in the appliqué.

7. Position the appliqué on the project.

No-sew Method Step 1: Apply a liquid fusible web around the edges of the appliqué *(Diagram D)*. Let dry. Speed the drying process with a hair dryer if desired.

> ### Note from Nancy
> Liqui Fuse Liquid Fusible Web is an ideal product to use to temporarily or even permanently attach appliqués. You can apply the gluelike liquid in a fine line, making it easier to create intricate designs.

No-sew Method Step 2: Place the appliqué on the project, positioning the background pieces on the design first and layering additional pieces to form the completed design. Cover with a press cloth; fuse the appliqué permanently in place. You don't need to do any stitching.

Stitching Method Step 1: Pin the appliqué to the base fabric, or use liquid fusible web to secure the appliqué.

Stitching Method Step 2: Position the background pieces first; then lay out the foreground pieces.

Stitching Method Step 3: Set the machine for a blindhem stitch with a length of 1.5 and a width of 2. Attach an embroidery or open toe foot. Insert a metafil needle and thread the needle with monofilament thread.

> ### Note from Nancy
> Always test machine settings on a fabric sample before stitching on a garment. You may need to adjust the stitch length, depending on how curved your appliqué edge is. The longer and straighter the edge, the longer the stitch length should be. You may also need to loosen the top tension so that the bobbin thread remains on the underside of the fabric.

Stitching Method Step 4: Stitch around the edges of the appliqué with the straight stitches falling on the base fabric at the edge of the appliqué and the zigzag stitches falling on the appliqué *(Diagram E)*. Because the thread is clear, the stitching is almost invisible.

> ### Note from Nancy
> An open toe foot has an extra-wide opening to make it easy to see the stitching area. This extra space is particularly helpful for blindhem stitching around an appliqué.

Invisibly Stitched Quilt Appliqués

This variation shows you how to stitch appliqués with points and corners. I chose a common quilt design, the six-pointed Morning Star, as the inspiration for this vest. I added the intertwining leaves using the same creative stitching technique.

Gather Supplies

Items listed on page 40, plus:
- ❑ Celtic Bias Bars
- ❑ Diamond-shaped template
- ❑ Quilting ruler
- ❑ Marking pencil
- ❑ Spray starch
- ❑ ¼"-wide (6 mm-wide) quilting foot (optional)

Select Fabrics

For the garment, choose fashion fabric. See your pattern for amount.

For star sections, choose an assortment of cotton or cotton blend scraps that coordinate with your fashion fabric.

For vines, choose an assortment of cotton or cotton blend scraps that contrast with your fashion fabric.

For lattice strips, choose black cotton or cotton blend scraps.

Get Ready

✔ Set up the sewing machine as detailed on page 40.

Create Vines and Lattice

1. Cut 1¼"-wide (3.2 cm-wide) black bias strips for the lattice.
2. Cut contrasting ¾"-wide (2 cm-wide) print bias strips for vines.
3. Fold strips wrong sides together, meeting lengthwise edges. Stitch narrow ⅛" (3 mm) seams (*Diagram A*).
4. Press tubes using Celtic Bias Bars.

Note from Nancy
Usually we stitch seams with fabric right sides together. This time we stitch with wrong sides together, since you will not turn the strips. If you find it difficult to stitch ⅛" (3 mm) seams, cut the strips slightly wider and stitch ¼" (6 mm) seams first. Then trim seams to ⅛" (3 mm) using a rotary cutter or scissors.

Note from Nancy
Celtic Bias Bars are flexible aluminum bars that make it easy to press fabric tubes. Stitchers may use the bars, which are available in various widths, to create Celtic (bias-strip appliqué) designs and for stained-glass quilting. I find these bars helpful when creating bias strips, such as the ones in this embellishment.

- Insert a Celtic Bias Bar in the tube.
- Position the seam at the center of one side of the bar.
- Finger-press the seam to one side; steam-press. (Metal bars get hot when you press, so be careful!) The pressed seam will stay on the underside of the tube when the tube is stitched to the garment.

Create Six-pointed Star Sections

1. Cut 1¾" (4.5 cm) fabric strips.
2. Make a diamond template using the pattern on page 138, and cut six sections for the six-pointed star using the template (Diagram B). Or cut diamonds using a quilting ruler specifically designed for creating a six-pointed star.
3. Prepare the fabric sections. Mark the starting and stopping points on the wrong side of each fabric section, ¼" (6 mm) from each corner. Be accurate, since these marks provide matching points when you join the sections. If you're using a template, poke a hole through the template at the seam intersection. Then use a marking pencil to transfer the position to the fabric (Diagram C).

   Spray-starch the fabric pieces to add body. This makes it easier to sew the sections together.
4. Join the fabric sections with ¼" (6 mm) seams, right sides together, beginning and ending at marks. Press the seam to one side (Diagram D).

Note from Nancy
If you quilt, you may have a ¼"-wide (6 mm-wide) quilting foot called the Little Foot in your accessory box. The ¼" (6 mm) width on the right side of the foot helps you keep a consistent seam allowance width.

5. Finish the outer edges of the pieced sections.
- Cut a rectangle of fusible interfacing slightly larger than the pieced section.
- Pin the pieced section to the interfacing, right sides together. (Fusible side of interfacing faces out.) Stitch completely around the outer edges with a ¼" (6 mm) seam. Trim the seam allowance to approximately ⅛" (3 mm); angle-cut corners (Diagram E).
6. Cut a slit in the center of the interfacing, taking care not to cut the appliqué fabric. Turn the appliqué right side out (Diagram F).

7. Use a tool with a rounded point to help obtain crisp edges on the appliqué. Roll the seam to the edge of the appliqué between your fingers and then press with the tip of the iron. The fusible interfacing adheres the two layers, giving sharp, crisp edges.
8. Stitch design to the garment.
- Position background sections such as lattice and stems first.
- Stitch around both outer edges following the techniques for Invisibly Stitched Appliqués on page 41 (Diagram G).
- Position foreground pieces (leaves and flowers) and stitch.

Invisibly Stitched Quilt Appliqué

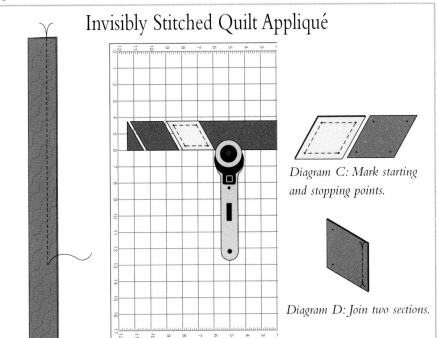

Diagram C: Mark starting and stopping points.

Diagram D: Join two sections.

Diagram A: Stitch narrow seams.

Diagram B: Use a template to cut star sections.

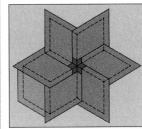

Diagram E: Stitch around outer edge of star.

Diagram F: Cut a slit; turn star right side out.

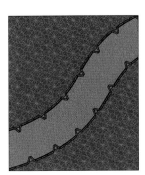

Diagram G: Stitch around outer edges.

Monogram

What do the letters, or fonts, on your computer have in common with sewing? A lot, when you use computer letters as stylized monograms to stitch on a project.

Gather Supplies

❑ Machine embroidery needle
❑ Machine embroidery thread
❑ Lingerie/bobbin thread
❑ Open toe or embroidery foot
❑ Gridded paper
❑ Tear-away or water-soluble stabilizer
❑ Ruler
❑ Appliqué scissors

Select Fabrics

Choose fashion fabric for your project. See your pattern for amount.

Choose contrasting or coordinating fabric for appliqué letters.

Get Ready

✔ Insert a machine embroidery needle in your machine.
✔ Thread the needle with machine embroidery thread and the bobbin with lingerie/bobbin thread.
✔ Replace the conventional foot with an open toe or embroidery foot.
✔ Loosen the upper tension by two positions or numbers (for example, from 5 to 3).
✔ Set the machine for a straightstitch with a short stitch length of 1.

Create Monogram Appliqués

1. Choose letters for the monogram using one of the following options:
• Use the alphabet on pages 140-141.
• Select letters from a printed alphabet, or print out letters using one of the fonts on a personal computer. Choose letters that are at least ¼" (6 mm) wide and styled without serifs (the

curved tails on some fonts). Serifs are difficult to appliqué.

2. Trace the letters on gridded paper, spacing the letters about ¼" (6 mm) apart *(Diagram A)*. If using letters from a personal computer, simply print out the name or monogram combination.

> ### Note from Nancy
> I like to use a gridded craft and pattern paper such as Grid Works™ when tracing letters to paper. This paper has a waxy backing, so you can press it to a base fabric to prevent the paper from shifting while you stitch. Added stabilization is a bonus.

3. Make a fabric sandwich.
• Place a layer of stabilizer on the underside of the fabric. Use either a tear-away stabilizer or a water-soluble stabilizer.

• For a centered monogram, fold the fashion fabric in half vertically; press to mark the center *(Diagram B)*. Position the fashion fabric over the stabilizer.
• Fold the fabric for the appliqué letters in half vertically; press to mark the center. If this fabric is lightweight, fuse a layer of lightweight fusible interfacing to the back of the fabric. Position this fabric over the fashion fabric, matching centers.
• Fold the paper with the traced or printed letters in half vertically to mark its center. Place the paper over the other layers, matching center marks *(Diagram C)*.
• Measure with a ruler to make certain the letters are aligned vertically and horizontally on the fashion fabric *(Diagram D)*. Once the letters are stitched, they're difficult to remove.

4. Straightstitch over each letter's traced outline through all four layers, using a short stitch length. Remove the paper after stitching around all letters *(Diagram E)*.

5. Trim the excess appliqué fabric, cutting very close to the stitching line, using one of the following techniques:
• Use conventional scissors. Bevel the blade by holding it flat against the fabric. Cut as close as possible to the stitching line, taking little snips as you trim around the curves *(Diagram F)*.
• Use appliqué scissors. The large bill lifts the fabric to be trimmed, and the curved handle ensures a comfortable hand position *(Diagram G)*.

6. Satin-stitch around the letters.
• Position the fabric so that the larger portion of the design is to the left of the machine.
• Adjust the machine for a narrow zigzag and a satin-stitch length of .5.
• Stitch so that one edge of the zigzag falls in the appliqué and the other edge falls just past the raw edge of it *(Diagram H)*.

Creating Monograms

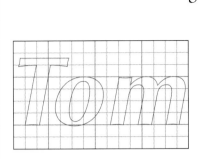

Diagram A: Trace letters on gridded paper.

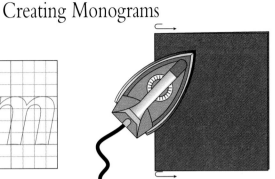

Diagram B: Fold and press fabric to mark center.

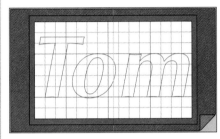

Diagram C: Match paper and fabric center marks.

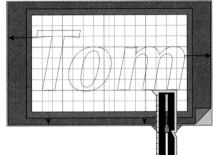

Diagram D: Use a ruler to check alignment of letters.

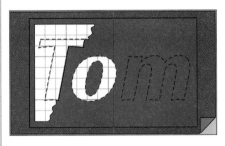

Diagram E: Straightstitch over each letter outline; remove paper.

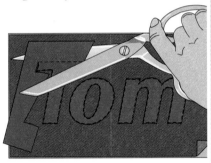

Diagram F: Trim excess appliqué fabric using conventional scissors.

Diagram G: Or use appliqué scissors to trim excess fabric.

Diagram H: Satin-stitch around edges of each letter.

• If possible, adjust the machine so that the needle stops in the down position for easy fabric turning.

• To stitch outside corners, zigzag to the corner, making sure the final stitch falls exactly at the corner *(Diagram I)*. Stop with the needle down in the outside position. Raise the presser foot and pivot the fabric. Lower the presser foot and continue stitching *(Diagram J)*.

• To stitch inside corners, stitch to the corner and then sew several additional stitches, sewing beyond the corner the width of a zigzag stitch *(Diagram K)*. Stop with the needle down in the inside position. Raise the presser foot and pivot the fabric. Lower the foot and continue stitching *(Diagram L)*.

• Give the fabric a little nudge when beginning a line of stitching that crosses previous stitching. Stitches can bunch up at those points, so helping the fabric along produces a smoother completed stitching.

7. Remove the stabilizer after you finish all stitching.

Creating Monograms, continued

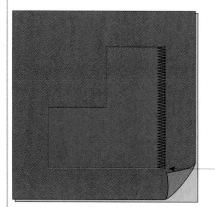

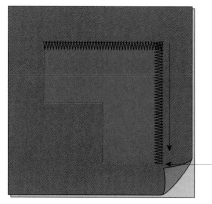

Diagram I: Make sure final stitch of an outside corner falls exactly at the corner.

Diagram J: Pivot; stitch the next side.

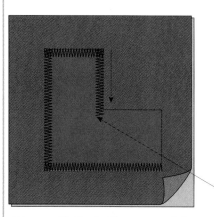

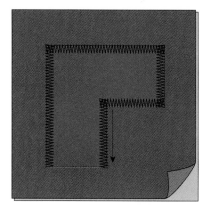

Diagram K: For inside corners, stitch beyond the corner the width of one zigzag stitch.

Diagram K: Pivot; stitch the next side.

Time-savers

If you use computer letters for your monograms, choose a sans serif (without serifs) typeface. Serifs are the short strokes on the ends of some styles of letters; these little strokes are difficult and timeconsuming to stitch around.

Choose a nonwoven or closely woven fabric for your monograms so that the fabric won't ravel. Ultrasuede and felt are good choices.

You can make felted wool from scraps or recycled clothing by washing the fabric in hot water and drying it on your dryer's hottest setting.

Be sure that the care instructions for monogram fabric you choose are compatible with the care instructions for your fashion fabric.

Confetti Appliqué

Cluster fabric scraps and add decorative stitching to create a unique look.

outline the area with a water-soluble marker to highlight the web, making it easier to see.

3. Using a rotary cutter and mat, cut fabric scraps into small pieces, varying the sizes and shapes.

4. Mound or cluster the confetti on the web. Add a few strands of embellishment thread if desired for interest. Cover with a press cloth and press *(Diagram A)*.

5. Dust off excess confetti (optional).

6. Zigzag randomly around the outer edges and over the entire piece to hold the tiny pieces in place *(Diagram B)*.

7. Change the machine stitch to a straightstitch and randomly stitch the area to add interest *(Diagram C)*.

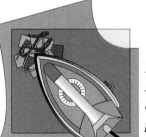

Diagram A: Arrange confetti on fusible web; press.

Diagram B: Zigzag randomly to hold tiny pieces in place.

Diagram C: Straightstitch over entire piece.

Gather Supplies

❑ Machine embroidery or metallic needle
❑ Machine embroidery thread or metallic thread for needle
❑ Thread that matches fashion fabric for bobbin
❑ Paper-backed fusible web
❑ Water-soluble fabric marker
❑ Rotary cutter and mat
❑ Press cloth

Select Fabrics

Choose a ready-made shirt or garment. Or choose a solid color fabric for your garment; see your pattern for amount.

Gather scraps of fabric that contrast or coordinate with the garment fabric.

Get Ready

✔ Insert a metallic or machine embroidery needle.
✔ Thread the needle with two strands of embroidery or metallic thread, threading as one strand.
✔ Use thread matching the fashion fabric in the bobbin.
✔ Set the machine for a medium length and medium width zigzag stitch.

Create Confetti Appliqués

1. Cut paper-backed fusible web into geometric shapes and press to garment in desired areas.

2. Remove the paper backing and

Folk Art Appliqués

Add a touch of folk art to your next project by using plaid fabric for appliqués.

Gather Supplies

❑ Size 90 machine embroidery needle
❑ Machine embroidery thread (two spools) for needle
❑ Thread that matches the fashion fabric for the bobbin
❑ Lightweight paper-backed fusible web
❑ Wave or pinking shears or rotary cutter and mat (optional)
❑ Decorative yarns
❑ Large hand-sewing needles
❑ Permanent marking pen (optional)
❑ Heavyweight paper-backed fusible web
❑ Tear-away stabilizer

Select Fabrics

Choose a solid color for the base fabric. See your pattern for amount.
Choose a plaid fabric for appliqués.

Get Ready

✔ Insert the embroidery needle in your machine.
✔ Thread the top of the machine with two strands of machine embroidery thread, threading both strands as one. Thread the bobbin with thread to match the fabric.
✔ Adjust the sewing machine for a wide blanket stitch. Test stitching on a fabric scrap.

Note from Nancy
If your machine does not have a programmed blanket stitch, use the blindhem stitch. Adjust the width and length of the stitch until it resembles a traditional blanket stitch.

✔ Loosen the top tension by two numbers or notches (for example, from 5 to 3).

Create Plaid Appliqués

1. Trace the appliqué design onto the paper side of lightweight web.
2. Roughly cut out the design; fuse the web to the wrong side of the plaid fabric *(Diagram A).*
3. Cut out the appliqué, following the traced design. For a folk art look, cut out the design using a wave or pinking blade *(Diagram B).*
4. Peel off the paper backing and fuse the appliqué to the project.
5. Stitch around the appliqués using one or several of the following techniques.

Running Stitch

1. Thread decorative yarn through a large-eyed hand-sewing needle.
2. Sew a running stitch ¼" (6 mm) inside the raw edges.
3. Knot threads on either the right side or the wrong side of the fabric. Knots exposed on the right side are characteristic of folk art techniques and provide an additional embellishment *(Diagrams C and D).*

Note from Nancy
Many decorative yarns are made of rayon. These yarns fray and are difficult to knot because the thread is slippery. Place a dab of a seam sealant, such as Fray Check, on the knot to prevent it from coming open (Diagram E). Dry the thread ends with the tip of the iron.

Pen Stitch

To "pen stitch," simply draw running stitches on fabric with a permanent fabric marking pen *(Diagram F)*. Since you don't secure pen-stitched appliqués with machine stitching, use a heavy-weight fusible web on your appliqués to provide a permanent no-sew bond.

Hand Blanket Stitch

1. Machine baste ¼" to ½" (6 mm to 1.3 cm) from edges of collars, pockets, and cuffs. This basting provides a stitching guide, which you will remove after you finish sewing.

2. Form a blanket stitch by anchoring the first stitch at the edge of the fabric.

3. Count over three or four basting stitches. For the next stitch and each succeeding one, insert the needle approximately ¼" (6 mm) from the fabric edge and ¼" (6 mm) from the preceding stitch, with the point of the needle toward you. Draw the point of the needle over the thread loop that forms *(Diagram G)*.

4. Repeat, always keeping the thread below the work and under the needle, forming a decorative thread along the project edge.

5. Remove the machine basting stitches when you finish the hand-stitching.

Machine Blanket Stitch

1. Back the fabric with a tear-away stabilizer.

2. Stitch with the straight stitches of the blanket stitch next to the outer edge of the appliqué and the zigzag stitches falling on the appliqué *(Diagram H)*.

Satin Stitch

1. Back the fabric with a stabilizer.

2. Set the machine for a satin stitch. Use only one thread in the top of the machine.

3. Stitch around the edges of the design *(Diagram I)*.

Creating Folk Art Appliqué

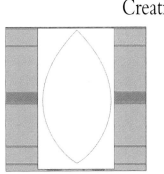

Diagram A: Fuse web to wrong side of fabric.

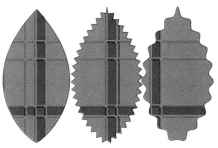

Diagram B: Cut appliqués as desired.

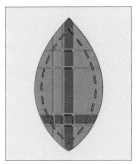

Diagram C: Sew a running stitch around raw edges.

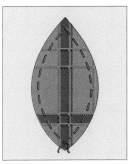

Diagram D: Leave knots on right side of fabric if desired.

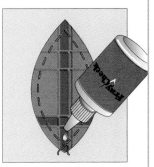

Diagram E: Apply seam sealant to knots.

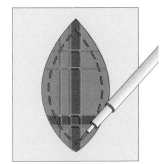

Diagram F: Draw running stitches using a fabric marker.

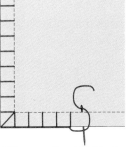

Diagram G: Add blanket stitches by hand.

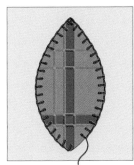

Diagram H: Sew blanket stitches by machine.

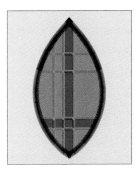

Diagram I: Satin-stitch appliqué edges.

Dimensional Appliqués

Instead of stitching one dimensional appliqués to your garment or project, make some of the appliqués look three-dimensional. It's a great folk art look.

Gather Supplies
❑ Paper-backed fusible web
❑ Buttons
❑ Embellishment yarns
❑ Large hand-sewing needles
❑ Machine embroidery thread for needle
❑ Thread that matches the fashion fabric for the bobbin

Create Dimensional Appliqués

1. Make square fringed flowers.
Cut two 2" (5 cm) squares of plaid for each flower.
• Fringe the edges of the squares, and then place them on top of each other, offsetting the top square to create the look of flower petals *(Diagram A)*.
• Cut a 1½" (3.8 cm) plaid circle and fuse it to the top square *(Diagram B)*.
• Finish the edges of the circle using one of the techniques described on pages 48 and 49.
• Sew buttons to the center of the circle. Tie threads on the top of the button circle, leaving thread tails as accents *(Diagram C)*.

2. Make round flowers.
• Using fusible web, cut and fuse a 1½" (3.8 cm) fabric circle for the center of the flower and two petal shapes, each 1½" (3.8 cm) in length *(Diagram D)*.
• Finish the edges of the appliqués using one of the techniques described on pages 48 and 49.
• Sew buttons around the outer edge of the circle, fastening the threads on the wrong side of the fabric *(Diagram E)*.
• Secure knots with a seam sealant if desired.

Making Appliqué Dimensional

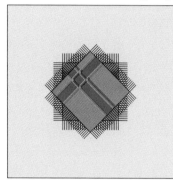

Diagram A: Place squares on top of each other, offsetting them.

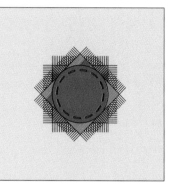

Diagram B: Fuse circle onto top square.

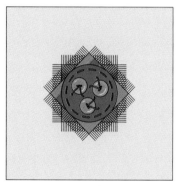

Diagram C: Sew buttons to "flower" center.

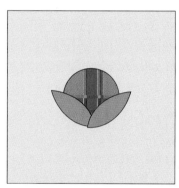

Diagram D: Fuse one circle and two leaves to make round flower.

Diagram E: Sew buttons around outer edge of flower.

Bias-Accent Appliqués

Combine bias strips with appliqués to simulate the look of stems and vines. What a simple yet interesting accent!

Gather Supplies

❏ Bias tape maker, ½" (1.3 cm) tape size
❏ Water-soluble basting tape

Create Bias-Accent Appliqués

1. Cut 1" (2.5 cm) bias strips of fabric.

2. Turn under the cut edges to form bias tape, using a bias tape maker. Insert the bias strip, wrong side up, through the wide end of the bias tape maker.

Using a safety pin or a straight pin, advance the fabric through the wide end of the tape maker. Fabric edges will fold to the middle as they come out the narrow end.

Press edges as they come from the tape maker.

Note from Nancy
To make bias tape without a bias tape maker, just press cut edges of a bias strip to the center (Diagram A).

3. Position the bias tape on the project using a water-soluble basting tape (Diagram B).

Note from Nancy
Wash-A-Way Basting Tape is ¼"-wide (6 mm-wide) water-soluble, double-sided tape. In difficult-to-pin areas, this product securely "bastes" fabric to fabric—an excellent notion to use when shaping the stems and vines of Folk Art Appliqués.

4. Stitch the bias to the project using one of the techniques described on pages 48 and 49.

Time-saver

For a true country look, eliminate the fusing from your appliqué. Without turning under raw edges, stitch the appliqués in place by hand or machine. The edges remain free.

Bias Appliqué

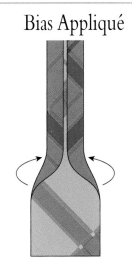

Diagram A: Press bias strip's cut edges to center.

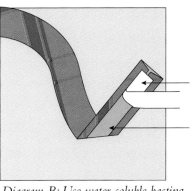

Diagram B: Use water-soluble basting tape to position bias tape.

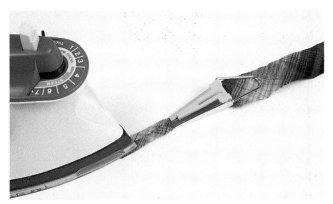

Bias Tape Maker

Fringed Buttonhole Appliqué

Add decorative buttonholes to fringed patches, and then highlight the patches with offset buttons. This makes an artistic combination of fabric, thread, and notions—something you can create, too!

Gather Supplies
❏ Lightweight fusible interfacing
❏ Rayon embroidery thread
❏ Machine embroidery needle
❏ Buttons

Select Fabrics
Choose fabric scraps to match your project, or use a coordinating or contrasting fabric for an accent.

Create Fringed Buttonhole Appliqués

1. Cut 1" to 1½" (2.5 cm to 3.8 cm) squares of woven fabric. Fringe the edges.

2. Stabilize the back of the buttonhole area with fusible interfacing.

3. Place the fringed rectangles on the project. You may want to pin them in place first until you're satisfied with the design.

4. Stitch buttonholes through all layers, using a machine embroidery needle and rayon embroidery thread. This lustrous thread adds another decorative element to the appliqué.

5. Add buttons, using the photo as a placement guide *(Diagram)*.

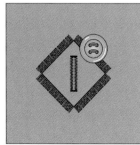

Add buttons to fringed appliqué.

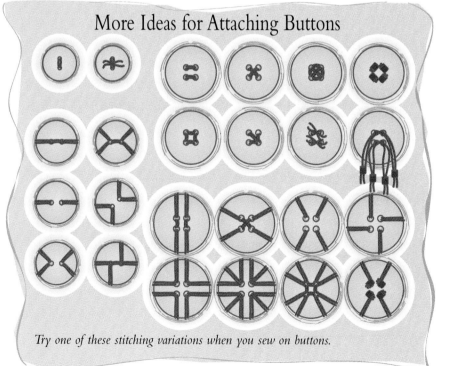

More Ideas for Attaching Buttons

Try one of these stitching variations when you sew on buttons.

Fringed Appliqués

Take advantage of a fabric's ability to ravel to add embellishments to projects.

Gather Supplies

Use the same supplies as for Fringed Buttonhole Appliqué on page 52.

Select Fabrics

Choose fabric scraps to match your project, or use a coordinating or contrasting fabric for an accent.

Create Fringed Appliqués

1. Cut fabric pieces for the appliqué, following the straight of grain. Geometric shapes, such as squares, rectangles, diamonds, and triangles, work best.

2. Fringe the outer edges of the shapes.

3. Add the fringed appliqués to the garment.

　Option 1: Insert the fringed shapes into seam lines.

　Option 2: Create a pseudo pin by combining a fringed section with several long threads. Fold fringed section or leave it flat as desired. Secure both to the garment with a button.

Time-savers

Take the time to plan your embellishment before you start sewing, and you'll save time in the long run. With fringed appliqué, for example, pin the appliqués into the seam line where you think you want them, and try on the garment section to see how they look. Then adjust the placement as needed. Stopping to try out the embellished garment takes less time than ripping out a seam and redoing it if you don't like the placement.

Some synthetic fabrics are not suitable for fringed appliqués because they ravel too much, and they wouldn't hold up in the laundry. If you're not sure how stable your fabric is, back the appliqué with fusible interfacing. Cut the interfacing the size and shape of your appliqué without the fringe.

Make a pseudo pin to embellish a purchased item. It's a quick way to personalize a denim jumper or a vest, using materials you already have in your sewing basket.

Cutwork Appliqué

You can create cutwork appliqué using a liquid fabric remover instead of cutting away the fabric.

Gather Supplies

❑ Size 90 (14) universal needle
❑ Open toe or embroidery foot
❑ 100% polyester or silk thread that matches or coordinates with the fashion fabric
❑ Tracing wheel and tracing paper
❑ Water-soluble stabilizer
❑ Liquid fabric remover

Select Fabrics

Choose a fabric with a plant origin (cotton, rayon, ramie, or linen). See your pattern for amount.

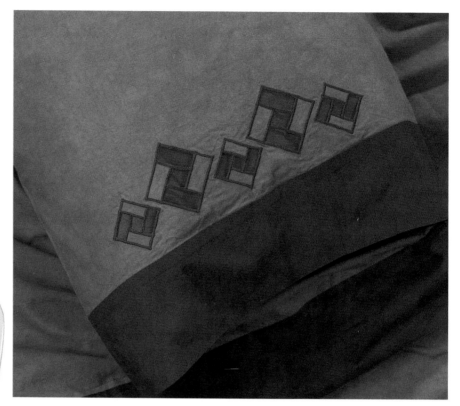

Note from Nancy

Common fabric removers, such as Fiber-Etch®, dissolve cotton, rayon, ramie, linen—all fibers of plant origin. To use this technique for cutwork, you must be sure that your fabric is plant-based and that your thread is not. It's critical to choose 100% polyester thread or silk thread in both the needle and bobbin when you use a liquid fabric remover. The non-plant-fiber thread acts as a barrier, keeping the liquid fabric remover from going beyond its intended boundaries.

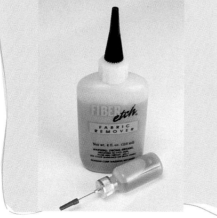

Get Ready

✔ Set the machine for a straightstitch.
✔ Insert a universal needle.
✔ Use a balanced thread tension.
✔ Replace the conventional presser foot with an open toe or embroidery foot.
✔ Use a 100% polyester or silk thread in both the bobbin and the needle of the machine.

Create Cutwork Appliqués

1. Choose an appliqué design that includes enclosed sections, or use the design on page 138.
2. Transfer the designs to the fabric using a tracing wheel and tracing paper.
3. Back the fabric with water-soluble stabilizer *(Diagram A)*.
4. Stitch around the traced designs with a straightstitch to ensure that the transfer markings do not rub off.
5. Set the machine for a satin stitch, using a stitch width of 3 and a stitch length of .5.

Note from Nancy

Make sure the stitches are not too narrow. This stitching establishes the boundaries of the design. If the stitches are too narrow, the liquid fabric remover may seep beyond them and dissolve fabric you need to keep.

6. Satin-stitch around the design, completely enclosing the area intended for the cutwork. Remove the stabilizer *(Diagram B)*.
7. Apply the liquid fabric remover within the enclosed areas next to the

satin stitching that will feature the cutwork. Let dry *(Diagram C)*.

8. Cover with a press cloth and press until the cutwork areas change color.

9. Remove the marked sections. If the sections do not fall out of their own accord, rinse the design under running water. Cutwork areas will drop out of the fabric, leaving a clean edge *(Diagram D)*.

Layered Cutwork

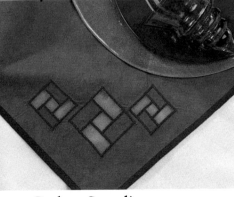

Gather Supplies

Use the same supplies listed for Cutwork Appliqué

Select Fabrics

Choose a fabric with a plant origin

Creating Cutwork Appliqué

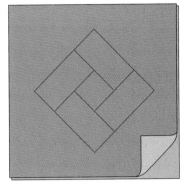

Diagram A: Trace designs onto fabric; back with water-soluble stabilizer.

Diagram B: Satin-stitch around design.

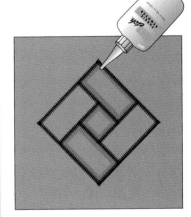

Diagram C: Apply liquid fabric remover.

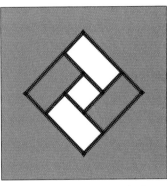

Diagram D: Remove marked sections.

(cotton, rayon, ramie, or linen) as the fashion fabric. See your pattern for amount.

Choose synthetic fabric of contrasting or coordinating color. This fabric will appear through the openings in the cutwork appliqué after you move the fashion fabric.

Get Ready

✔ Use the same machine set-ups listed for Cutwork Appliqué.

Create Layered Cutwork

1. Transfer the design to the right side of the fashion fabric using a tracing wheel and tracing paper *(Diagram)*.

2. Behind the traced area, stack the fabrics in the following order: stabilizer on the bottom, synthetic fabric in the middle (right side up), and fashion fabric on top (right side up).

3. Follow steps 4 through 6 under Cutwork Appliqué. When you remove the fashion fabric portions, the synthetic fabric underneath appears.

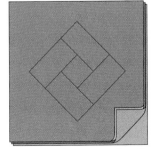

Diagram: Transfer design to right side of fabric.

Ultrasuede Appliqué

Nonravelling Ultrasuede is the perfect accent for appliqué projects.

Gather Supplies
- ❑ Metafil needle
- ❑ Monofilament nylon thread
- ❑ Lightweight paper-backed fusible web
- ❑ Press cloth
- ❑ Lightweight stabilizer

Select Fabrics
Choose a ready-made garment or fashion fabric. See your pattern for amount.

Use Ultrasuede fabric or scraps for appliqué shapes.

Get Ready
- ✔ Insert a Metafil needle in your machine.
- ✔ Thread the top of the machine with monofilament nylon thread.
- ✔ Adjust the machine for a blindhem stitch with a length of 1.5 and a width of 2.

Create Ultrasuede Appliqués
1. Position the appliqués.

Note from Nancy
Check the references on page 19 for fusible webs—they are not all alike! I recommend lightweight fusible web to combine with Ultrasuede. The heat and moisture of an iron have a hard time penetrating Ultrasuede. Lighter web melts more readily than traditional fusible web, making it a better match for Ultrasuede.

- • Trace the appliqué design on the paper side of the fusible web.
- • Press the fusible web to the Ultrasuede fabric and cut out the design.
- • Position the design on the project. Cover with a press cloth and lightly fuse.
- • Flip the project so that the right side faces the ironing board. Finish the fusing process.

Note from Nancy
Always do the final fusing from the wrong side when working with Ultrasuede. With the suede protected by the ironing board, you won't flatten the nap and create an iron imprint. Play it safe—press from the wrong side!

2. Back the fabric with a lightweight stabilizer.

3. Stitch the appliqué onto the garment, using the blindhem stitch; or simply edgestitch the design with a straightstitch.

Note from Nancy
If using the blindhem stitch, test stitch length and width on a sample, adjusting to accommodate the shape of the appliqués. Stitch so that the straightstitch runs along the edge of the appliqué and the zigzag of the blindhem stitch catches the appliqué.

Appliqué Collar Band

You can personalize or upgrade a plain purchased shirt by adding Ultrasuede. Stitch distinctive accents at the collar band, pocket and yoke.

Gather Supplies

In addition to the general supplies for Ultrasuede Appliqués, you need:

❑ Purchased shirt
❑ Tissue paper
❑ Tracing wheel (optional)
❑ Thread that matches the Ultrasuede and the shirt

Select Fabrics

Choose Ultrasuede for appliqués:

• 9" x 12" (23 cm x 30.5 cm) square for collar
• Scraps for designs

Create an Appliqué Collar Band

1. Create a pattern for the collar band, taking the pattern from the shirt itself.

• Place a layer of tissue paper, wider and longer than the collar band, on a padded surface.

• Position the shirt flat on top of the tissue paper, placing the center of the collar band at the center of the paper. Mold the fabric to meet the paper, making the collar as flat as possible.

• Transfer the collar band shape to the paper by poking a needle along the

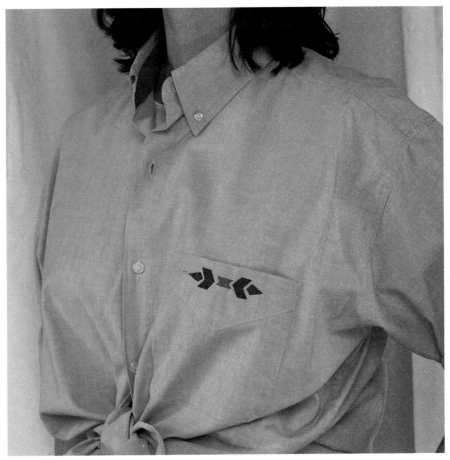

shirt seam line or tracing with a tracing wheel, piercing holes in the paper. You may have to do one section of the collar and then reposition the shirt to do another section.

• Connect the pierced dots with a pencil. If you prefer, you can make a pattern for half the collar, and then cut out the traced section on the fold to get a full pattern.

2. Cut out the collar band from Ultrasuede, using the newly created pattern.

Note from Nancy
Another fabric option is Ultraleather™. As the name implies, this fabric combines the feel and appearance of real leather with the easy-care qualities of a synthetic fabric.

3. Remove the button from the shirt collar band.

4. Pin the new collar band to the inside of the original collar band. Edgestitch in place using either monofilament nylon thread or thread that matches the collar band and shirt.

5. Attach the button to the collar band.

6. Prepare and apply appliqués from scraps, following instructions on page 56 *(Diagram)*.

Diagram: Use Ultrasuede scraps for pocket appliqués.

Framed-Stitch Appliqué

Take an ordinary satin-stitched appliqué and make it dramatic by outlining the satin stitches with metallic thread.

Gather Supplies

❑ Machine embroidery needle
❑ Rayon machine embroidery thread to contrast with fashion fabric and appliqué
❑ Lingerie/bobbin thread or a thread to match the fabric
❑ Embroidery or open toe foot
❑ Lightweight stabilizer
❑ Metafil needle
❑ Metallic thread

Select Fabrics

For garment, choose a fashion fabric. Check your pattern for amount.

For appliqué, choose Ultrasuede fabric in a color that complements your fashion fabric.

Get Ready

✔ Insert machine embroidery needle. You'll replace it later with the Metafil needle.
✔ Thread the needle with machine embroidery thread.
✔ Use lingerie/bobbin thread or thread that matches the fabric in the bobbin.
✔ Set the machine for a satin stitch using a wide width. I used a stitch width of 4 and a stitch length of .5.
✔ Loosen the top tension by two numbers (for example, from 5 to 3).
✔ Replace the conventional foot with an embroidery or open toe foot.

Create Framed-Stitch Appliqué

1. Apply your Ultrasuede appliqué design to your garment, using the method described on page 56.
2. Back the appliqué area with a stabilizer. Satin-stitch around the outside edges of the appliqué *(Diagram A)*.
3. Replace the embroidery needle with the Metafil needle. Thread the needle with metallic thread.
4. Set the machine for a triple stitch. Built into most sewing machines, this stitch takes two stitches forward and one stitch back. Select a regular stitch length.
5. Stitch around both edges of the satin stitching, forming a frame *(Diagram B)*.

Framed-Stitch Appliqué

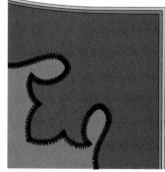

Diagram A: Satin-stitch around outside edges.

Diagram B: Straightstitch around both edges of satin stitching.

Ultrasuede Buttonhole Appliqué

Change an off-the-rack shirt into a one-of-a-kind creation by adding simple Ultrasuede appliqués over the buttonhole area.

Gather Supplies
❑ In addition to the general supplies listed under Ultrasuede Appliqué, you need paper.

Select Fabrics
Choose a ready-made garment, or buy fashion fabric and pattern. See your pattern for amount of fabric.

Choose Ultrasuede fabric for appliqués.

Get Ready
✔ Thread the needle with metallic or monofilament thread.
✔ Use thread to match the garment in the bobbin.
✔ Set the machine for a straightstitch.

Note from Nancy
Sometimes, the time-consuming part of the sewing process is deciding which design to use. Look through books for ideas, or create shapes of your own. Cut shapes from paper, and position them on the garment to see if you like the effect. I find geometric and abstract shapes very attractive for this creative embellishment.

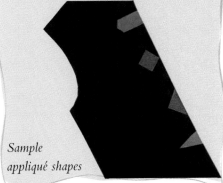

Sample appliqué shapes

Create Buttonhole Appliqué
1. Select an appliqué for the buttonhole area.
2. To position all elements correctly, make a test buttonhole using the appliqué and garment fabrics. If you can't use actual garment fabric, use a fabric of similar weight and color from your fabric stash.
3. Attach the appliqué using your favorite technique outlined earlier *(Diagrams A and B)*.

4. If you are stitching the appliqué to a ready-made garment, open the buttonhole after you finish the appliqué.
• Poke pins through the ends of the existing buttonholes to mark starting and stopping points *(Diagram C)*.
• Using a pair of small scissors, carefully open the buttonhole through the appliqué fabric, working from the right side of the fabric.
• Stitch around the buttonhole with a straightstitch or satin stitch.

Ultrasuede Buttonhole Appliqué

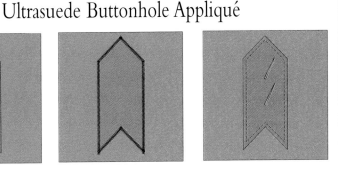

Diagram A: Straightstitch appliqué in place.

Diagram B: Or zizag or satinstitch appliqué in place.

Diagram C: Use pins to mark buttonhole placement.

Ultrasuede Toggles

Add an interesting design and create a closure in one simple yet creative step by making Ultrasuede toggles.

Gather Supplies
❑ Metafil needle
❑ Monofilament nylon thread
❑ Lightweight paper-backed fusible web
❑ Press cloth
❑ Lightweight stabilizer

Select Fabrics
Choose a ready-made garment or fashion fabric. See your pattern for amount.

Use Ultrasuede fabric or scraps for appliqué shapes.

Get Ready
✔ Insert a Metafil needle in your machine.
✔ Thread the top of the machine with monofilament nylon thread.

Create Toggles
1. Trace appliqué designs on the paper side of the fusible web. Abstract shapes or simple geometric shapes like the triangles pictured work well. Press fusible web to the Ultrasuede fabric and cut out the designs.
2. Pin the appliqué shapes on each side of the closure.
3. Cut narrow strips of suede 6" (15 cm) long.
4. Place the strips (one or more per side) under the center edge of the appliqués. Fuse the appliqués in place to serve as ties *(Diagram)*.
5. Stitch the appliqués in place using a straightstitch.
6. Tie knots or add beads to the ends of the suede ties.

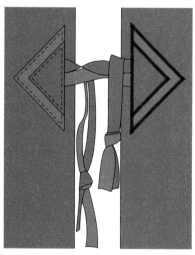

Diagram: Fuse appliqués over tie strips.

Other ideas

Toggle Closure for a Handbag

Cutwork Applique Lapel

Confetti Applique on a Bodice

Ultrasuede Buttonhole Appliques

Put odd-sized fabric scraps to good use by crazy-quilting jacket lapels *(left and page 68)*. Wind bobbins and use these on a thread palette for small sections of serged patchwork *(page 67).*

When you sew patchwork, you actually create fabric. Embellish one area or stitch an entire garment using your new fabric.

Wearable Patchwork

Combine decorative stitching, pleats, and other techniques to make a delicate Heirloom Patchwork blouse *(left and page 80)*. Show off your serged seams by putting them on the outside of a Serged Patchwork vest *(right and page 66).*

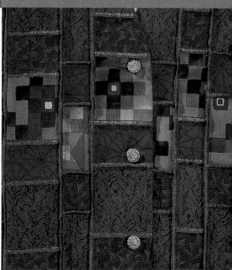

Add a Plaid Pinwheel block to the front of a jumper *(left and page 74)* or the back of a jacket, or make a slightly larger Plaid Pinwheel for a wall hanging *(page 76)*.

Fusible Patchwork
Vest, page 64

Fusible Patchwork

This embellishment is a great technique for beginners—you don't sew any seams!

Gather Supplies

❑ Fabric-marking pen
❑ Medium-weight fusible interfacing
❑ 4.0/90 double needle
❑ Thread
❑ Pinking shears or rotary cutter with a wave blade or a pinking blade and cutting mat
❑ Press cloth

Select Fabrics

For patchwork, use coordinating fabrics that are compatible in weight and care. Consider interlock knits, cottons, and synthetic suede, such as Ultrasuede and Ultrasuede Lite.

Buy narrow trim or create trim from a nonraveling fabric, such as interlock knit or synthetic suede.

Get Ready

✔ Set machine for a medium-width zigzag stitch.
✔ Use matching thread in needle and bobbin.

Create Fusible Patchwork

1. From fusible interfacing, cut the pattern pieces you plan to embellish, eliminating armhole, front, and lower-edge seam allowances *(Diagram A)*. Use light-colored interfacing with light-colored fabrics and dark interfacing with dark fabrics.

2. Use a fabric-marking pen to mark vertical and horizontal lines to serve as alignment points.
• Mark the center of the interfacing piece, following the lengthwise grain.
• Mark one horizontal line at right angles to the center line *(Diagram B)*.
• Place interfacing on ironing board, fusible side up.

Note from Nancy

If your vest will have bias-bound edges like the denim one I made, trim the seam allowances from the outer edges of the front interfacing section and the back pattern piece. You only need the shoulder and side seams (Diagram A).

3. Cut 3" (7.6 cm) squares of coordinating fabrics. I used 3" (7.5 cm) squares in the denim vest. Since the fabrics completely cover the interfacing foundation, you can use any size patchwork.

4. Arrange the squares on the interfacing, using marked lines as positioning guides. Place squares so their edges meet. Some of the squares will extend beyond the edge of the interfacing *(Diagram C)*.

5. Cover fabric squares with a press cloth. Following interfacing manufacturer's instructions, fuse with an iron, repositioning the iron until the entire piece is fused *(Diagram D)*.

Note from Nancy

If you do not use a press cloth, any fusible interfacing not covered by fabric may end up on the bottom of your iron. If you use synthetic suede, test pressing on a sample to ensure that the heat of the iron does not flatten the nap.

Making Fusible Patchwork

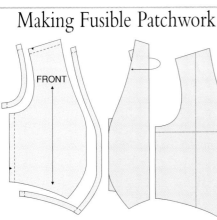

Diagram A: Eliminate pattern seam allowances.

Diagram B: Mark horizontal and vertical lines.

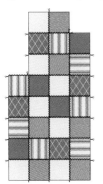

Diagram C: Arrange squares on interfacing.

Diagram D: Fuse entire piece.

Diagram E: Zizag along all edges.

Diagram F: Place strips on vertical seams.

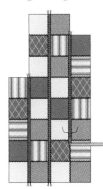

Diagram G: Stitch trim in place.

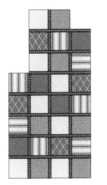

Diagram H: Place and stitch horizontal strips.

Stitching Options

Quick-Stitch Trim

6a. Zigzag along the lengthwise and crosswise edges of the squares with a long, wide stitch *(Diagram E)*. You won't see this stitching on the completed vest; it merely keeps the edges flat and makes it easier to apply the trim.

7a. Add trim to seams.

• Cut ½" (1.3 cm) strips of knit. You can cut the strip edges straight, wavy, or pinked, as you prefer. I cut the edges of the trim on the pictured vest using a rotary cutter with a pinking blade. I could have used pinking shears or a rotary cutter with a wave blade.

Rotary cutter with wave blade

• Position strips over lengthwise square intersections, covering the seams *(Diagram F)*.

• Insert the double needle. Thread both the needles and the bobbin with thread that matches the trim. Stitch the trim to the fusible patchwork *(Diagram G)*. As an option, straight-stitch along both edges of the strip using a single needle in your sewing machine.

• Repeat, positioning and stitching trim over crosswise square intersections *(Diagram H)*.

8a. Treat the newly created fusible patchwork as fabric. My denim vest is lined, and the edges are bound with bias strips of fabric.

Decorative Stitching

6b. Set up machine for decorative stitching.

• Insert a machine embroidery needle if you're using rayon thread; insert a metallic needle if using metallic thread.

• Thread the top of the machine with rayon or metallic thread; use all-purpose thread that matches the fabric in the bobbin.

• Adjust the machine for a decorative stitch and attach an embroidery foot.

• Loosen the top tension by two numbers or notches.

> *Note from Nancy*
> *If you use synthetic suede for your patchwork, you can be especially creative in adding decorative stitching to the seamlines. With fabric that ravels, you'll need to use a dense decorative stitch, covering the seams completely. Since synthetic suede doesn't ravel, you can choose airy or dense decorative stitches. The choice is yours!*

7b. Stitch over the butted edges of patchwork with a decorative stitch.

8b. Follow instructions in **8a.**

Time-savers

🕐 Use fused patchwork on one pattern piece only, such as one side of a vest, using a coordinating solid-color fabric for the other side and the back.

🕐 Cut larger fabric squares (but remember to keep your squares in proportion to your overall finished project).

🕐 Use the decorative stitching option for finishing. You save the time of cutting and applying the quick-stitch trim.

Serged Patchwork

Use your serger to create exciting patchwork.

Note from Nancy

Add interest to the stitching by blending several threads in each looper. To make this process easier, place a thread palette on a looper thread spindle, and feed two threads through each looper tension guide, treating them as a single thread. A thread palette is a plastic stand designed to fit over your serger spool holder. It feeds thread from up to five spools into the upper or lower loopers of your serger. You can also place the palette over a sewing machine cone thread stand to feed up to three types of thread into the upper part of your sewing machine.

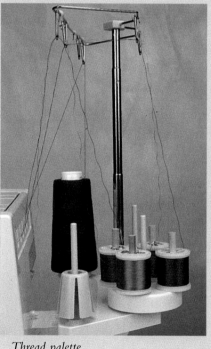

Thread palette

Gather Supplies

❑ For the upper and lower loopers, two spools each of rayon machine embroidery thread in two coordinating colors that highlight the fabrics

❑ For the needle, all-purpose serger thread that matches the fabric

❑ Thread palette

Select Fabrics

Choose two coordinating 100%-cotton, medium-weight fabrics with a small design.

Choose two 100%-cotton, medium-weight fabrics with a large design, in a color and style that are compatible with the first two.

Get Ready

✔ Adjust the serger for a balanced 3-thread overlock stitch, with normal stitch width and a short stitch length.

✔ Thread two coordinating rayon threads in both the upper and lower loopers; thread all-purpose serger thread in the needle.

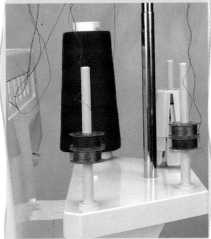

Bobbins replacing thread cones

Create Serged Patchwork

1. Cut 2½" to 3" (6.3 cm to 7.5 cm) crosswise strips of each large print and 1½" to 2" (3.8 cm to 5 cm) crosswise strips of each small print.

2. Serge the strips together.

• Match two strips of different widths, wrong sides together. Serge lengthwise edges *(Diagram A)*. The seam is exposed on the fabric's right side.

• Join additional strips in a random layout, alternating strip sizes and colors until the serged fabric is slightly longer than the pattern section.

• Press serged seams in one direction, pressing from the right side because seams are exposed.

3. Recut the newly formed serged strips (called "strata") crosswise into various sections ranging in width from 1" to 3" (2.5 cm to 7.5 cm). Vary widths to add interest *(Diagram B)*. Do not cut sections narrower than 1" (2.5 cm) or they will be too small after pieces are serged back together.

4. Serge the sections together.

• Invert one section; match it to a second section, wrong sides together. To accentuate a patchwork design, slightly offset the strips. Place the section with the seam allowances pressed upward on top *(Diagram C)*.

• Serge, using a small screwdriver, stiletto, or a Puts-it to keep the seams facing the correct direction.

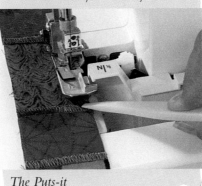

The Puts-it

• Add more sections, varying strip widths and inverting every other section, until you've created sufficient fabric to cut out pattern pieces *(Diagram D)*.

• Repeat for the other vest front. You don't have to create a mirror image of the design. The arrangement should be fun and free flowing.

5. Cut out the pattern pieces. Complete the project following your pattern instructions.

Creating Serged Patchwork

Diagram A: Serge 2 strips together.

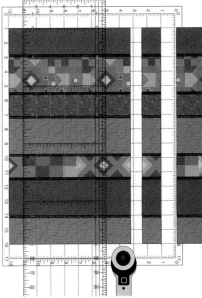

Diagram B: Cut serged strips into sections.

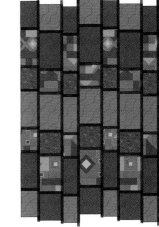

Diagram C: Serge 2 sections together.　　*Diagram D: Continue adding sections.*

Crazy Patchwork with Decorative Stitching

This jacket spotlights an attractive use of fabric scraps as well as dramatic highlights of metallic threads.

Gather Supplies
- All-purpose thread
- Metallic thread(s)
- Metallic needle, size 80 (12)
- Quilting ruler or 6" quilting square, or plastic template sheets
- Embroidery foot

Select Fabrics

Collect scraps of similar colors, or coordinate colored scraps of various cotton fabrics.

Buy 100%-cotton flannel or muslin to use as a stabilizer for the patchwork section.

Note from Nancy
Use flannel as a stabilizer to create interesting texture. After decoratively stitching the patchwork to flannel, wash the fabric. Flannel made from 100% cotton shrinks, adding dimension to patchwork.

Get Ready
- ✔ Set machine for a straightstitch.
- ✔ Use all-purpose thread in the needle and the bobbin that coordinates with the fabric scraps.

Create Crazy Patchwork

1. Cut fabric for crazy quilt blocks.
- For block centers, cut numerous polygon-shaped pieces with sides approximately 2" to 3" (5 cm to 7.5 cm). The number depends on the size of the finished project *(Diagram A)*. I cut 12 center sections for my jacket.
- Cut the remaining scraps into strips of various widths.

2. Stitch crazy quilt blocks using an adaptation of a Log Cabin technique.
- Place a center section on one of the fabric strips, right sides together, aligning one edge of the center section along the strip. Repeat, placing additional center sections along the strip. Allow space between center sections to provide room for cutting the strip into separate segments. *(Diagram B)*.
- Stitch the center sections to the strip with a narrow seam allowance.
- Open the fabric so that the right side faces up. Press or finger-press seam allowances in one direction.
- Cut the strips apart, extending and cutting along the line of the center section *(Diagram C)*.
- Place a second fabric strip on the bed of the sewing machine, right side up. Align the crazy pieces along one edge of that strip, right sides together, to determine spacing; again allow extra fabric between sections for angle

cuts. Stitch the strips together *(Diagram D)*. Open the fabrics so that right sides face up. Press seam allowances in one direction.

• Cut the sections following the angle of the crazy piece.

• Add subsequent strips so that the crazy piece forms a square shape. The shape will not be perfectly square, but you will trim it to the correct size and shape.

3. Cut a 6" (15 cm) template or use a 6"-square quilting ruler or a rotary-cutting ruler to trim crazy pieces to that size *(Diagram E)*.

Use your creativity in cutting these squares. Cant or tilt your template to cut some squares at an angle. Use larger squares (up to about 8" or 20.5 cm). Cut squares according to your personal preference.

4. Combine crazy quilt blocks to make fabric for your project.

• Seam the squares together to create a patchwork piece slightly larger than the pattern piece.

• Back the squares with a piece of 100%-cotton muslin or flannel (wrong sides facing) before you add decorative stitches, or use a stabilizer *(Diagram F)*.

5. Set up the machine for decorative stitching.

• Insert a metallic needle.

• Attach an embroidery foot.

• Use all-purpose thread to match your fabric in the bobbin and contrasting metallic thread in the needle to emphasize the stitches.

• Loosen the top tension by two numbers or notches.

6. Embellish the patchwork with decorative stitches.

• Select one or more decorative stitches. Stitch along seams of the crazy patchwork to embellish. This is an ideal project for a beginner. Just doodle at the machine, playing with the decorative stitches on the fabric like you might doodle with a pen on paper.

• Randomly stitch design(s) along the seams of the crazy piecing *(Diagram G)*.

• Change threads and stitch patterns as desired.

7. Wash the fabric. This causes the muslin or flannel layer to shrink and create attractive puckering.

8. Cut out the pattern shapes and construct the garment following your pattern instructions.

Stitching Crazy Patchwork

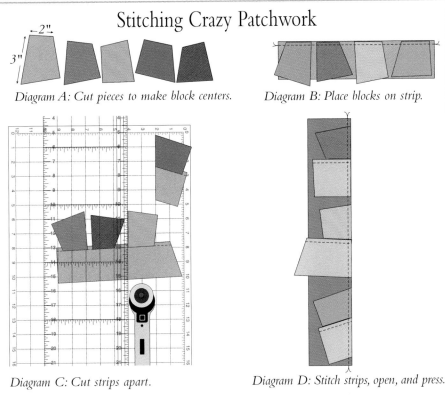

Diagram A: Cut pieces to make block centers.

Diagram B: Place blocks on strip.

Diagram C: Cut strips apart.

Diagram D: Stitch strips, open, and press.

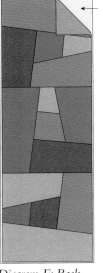

Diagram E: Trim crazy pieces to size.

Diagram F: Back squares with stabilizer.

Diagram G: Use decorative stitches to sew.

Dimensional Patchwork

Use three different patchwork techniques to make this blouse, or try any one of them to make a pillow or a wall hanging.

Gather Supplies
❑ All-purpose thread
❑ Nylon thread
❑ Universal needle
❑ Metafil needle
❑ Rotary cutter, mat, and ruler

Select Fabric
Choose a base color; check your pattern for amount.

Buy ¼ yard (23 cm) each of two contrasting fabrics.

Get Ready
✔ Set up your sewing machine for a straightstitch and insert the universal needle.
✔ Use all-purpose thread in the needle and bobbin that coordinates with all fabrics.

Create Quarter-Circles
1. Cut circles and squares.

• Cut four 3" (7.5 cm) squares from the base fabric.
• Cut eight 3½" (9 cm) circles from contrasting fabric (two for each square).

Note from Nancy
Our instructions make 2½" (6.3 cm) finished squares. For other dimensions, be sure your circle diameter is ½" (1.3 cm) larger than your base square. For a 4" (10 cm) base square, cut 4½" (11.5 cm) circles.

2. Create quarter-circles.
• Join two circles, right sides together. Stitch around the outer edge with a ¼" (6 mm) seam.
• Nip the seam allowances (make ¼" or 6 mm clips) without cutting the stitching line. Or use pinking shears to grade and clip in one operation *(Diagram A)*.

• Fold the circle in half; press to mark. Fold in half again; press to mark the circle into quarters.
• Cut the circle into quarters along pressed lines. Turn each quarter right side out. Roll the edges with your fingers to get the seam exactly on the edge. Press *(Diagram B)*.
3. Position four quarter-circles on the right side of each base square, meeting the circle's cut edges to the square's corners. Machine-baste ⅛" (3 mm) from the edges *(Diagram C)*.

Creating Quarter-Circles

Diagram A: Nip seams or use pinking shears to grade seam.

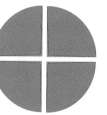

Diagram B: Cut circle into quarters and turn right side out.

Diagram C: Place quarter-circles on base square.

Create Quilting Strips

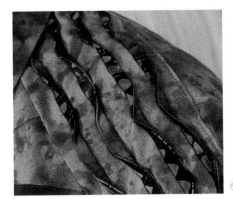

This quilting idea is a little more complex and requires more time than the previous technique, but the results are spectacular! Insert tucks of contrasting fabric between strips of the base fabric, then add directional stitching to produce this dramatic result.

1. Cut strips to make twists.

• Cut five 1¼" (3.2 cm) crosswise strips from base fabric.

• Cut four ¾" (2 cm) crosswise strips of each of *two* contrasting fabrics (eight strips total).

2. Stitch the twist strips.

• Meet ¾" (2 cm) strips of the contrasting fabrics, right sides together.

• Stitch one long edge with a ¼" (6 mm) seam; press *(Diagram D)*.

• Turn strip right side out, meeting cut edges.

• Repeat, stitching and pressing all four twist strips.

> ### Note from Nancy
> To get a sharp crease at the edge where the two fabrics are seamed, first press the seam flat and then press it open. This makes it much easier to position the stitching line precisely at the fold when you turn the strip right side out.

3. Join the twist and base strips.

• Place two base strips right sides together and sandwich a twist strip between them, meeting cut edges. Stitch a ¼" (6 mm) seam *(Diagram E)*.

• Repeat until all the twist strips and the base strips are stitched together *(Diagram F)*.

• Press all seams in one direction.

> ### Note from Nancy
> For the strips to twist, you must join each strip to a base strip with the same fabric facing up. Before you stitch, be sure that the same side of each twist faces the same direction.

4. Mark and stitch the twists.

• Square the end of the strip. Measure and mark a series of lines 1½" (3.8 cm) apart. Vary this measurement if you wish. For example, draw all lines only 1" (2.5 cm) apart to make twists more definite.

• Insert a Metafil needle and thread the needle with nylon thread. Match the bobbin thread to the fabric.

• Straightstitch the twists to the fabric, stitching from top to bottom on the first row and from bottom to top on the second row. Repeat, alternating stitching direction on each row *(Diagram G)*.

Making Quilting Strips

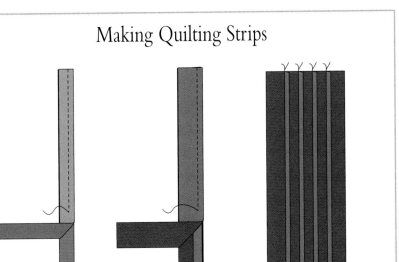

Diagram D: Stitch 1 long edge of strip.

Diagram E: Sandwich 1 twist between 2 base strips.

Diagram F: Join all twist and base strips.

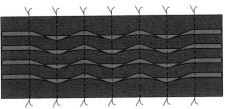

Diagram G: Alternate stitching direction in each row.

Create Dimensional Right Triangles

1. Cut eight 3" (7.5 cm) squares from the base fabric.
2. Make right triangles from contrasting fabric.
• Cut eight 3" (7.5 cm) squares from the second contrasting fabric.
• Fold each contrasting square in half diagonally, wrong sides together, to create a right triangle *(Diagram H)*.
3. Place each right triangle on the right side of a base square, meeting cut edges. Machine-baste ⅛" (3 mm) from the edges *(Diagram I)*.

Making Dimensional Right Triangles

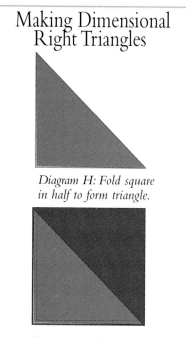

Diagram H: Fold square in half to form triangle.

Diagram I: Place triangle on base square and baste.

Put It All Together

The instructions tell you how I created the pieced fabric used for the purple-and-green blouse, but you can create other designs with the same pieces. Place the finished blocks on a flat surface and move them around until you're pleased with the look.

1. Arrange the quilt blocks.
• Meet four quarter-circles to create the center of the design.
• Place two dimensional triangles at each side, the top, and the bottom of the center square.
• Cut four 3" (7.5 cm) squares from the fabric you used to make the quarter-circles. Place these in the corners *(Diagram J)*.
• Cut the twist strip into blocks the length you want and arrange them along the quilt block sides. Mine are 10½" x 3½" (27 cm x 9 cm).
• Cut squares of contrasting fabric as needed to fill in the corners of your block. I used 3½" (9 cm) squares.
2. Assemble the block center (without the twist strips and outside corner blocks). *Use ¼" (6 mm) seam allowances throughout.*
• Join adjacent pairs of segments for the center portion, chain-piecing them together *(Diagram K)*.
• Join the paired segments to form vertical rows, chain-piecing them *(Diagram L)*.
• Press seams on adjacent blocks in opposite directions. This reduces bulk when seaming the horizontal rows.
• Join the horizontal seams, placing vertical rows with right sides together and matching seam intersections. Since the blocks are chain-pieced together like a honeycomb, matching is easy *(Diagram M)*.

4. Add the twist-strip border.
• Place a twist strip at each side of the block center, right sides together.
• Stitch a corner block to each end of the remaining two twist strips, right sides together.
• Place the remaining twist strips at the top and bottom of the block, matching seams, and stitch *(Diagram N)*.
6. Use the dimensional patchwork as part of your next sewing project.

Joining Dimensional Patchwork Blocks

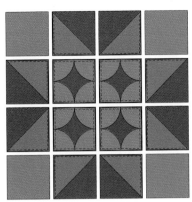

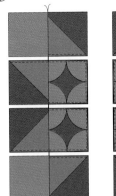

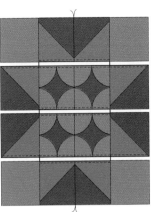

Diagram J: Arrange quilt blocks for center portion.

Diagram K: Join adjacent pairs of segments.

Diagram L: Join paired segments to form vertical rows.

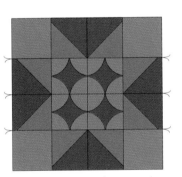

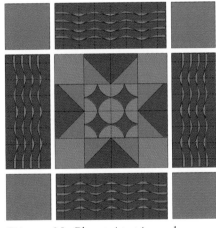

Diagram M: Join horizontal seams.

Diagram N: Place twist strips and corners around center block.

Diagram O: Cut the block diagonally to duplicate blouse on page 70.

More Ideas

Jumper bib

Wall hanging

Pillow top

Plaidwork

Instead of using calicos and prints for patchwork, try plaids in traditional quilt patterns. I made Pinwheels, Seminole piecing, and Courthouse Steps.

Select Fabrics

Choose equal yardage of two plaid fabrics and two coordinating solid-colored fabrics. For the pictured jumper, we used ⅛ yard (11.5 cm) of each fabric. Make sure one of your plaid fabrics has a dominant stripe.

Buy additional fabric for the back of the Pinwheel block and for completion of your project as your pattern requires.

Get Ready

✔ Set up your sewing machine for a straightstitch. Use thread in the needle and the bobbin that coordinates with all fabrics.

✔ Attach a foot that provides a guide for stitching a ¼" (6 mm) seam allowance.

✔ Or set up your serger for a 4-thread overlock stitch. Set seam width for ¼" (6 mm) and use all-purpose serger thread.

> ### Note from Nancy
> You need to maintain an accurate seam width. If your machine allows it, adjust your needle position so that it is precisely ¼" (6 mm) from the cut edges. Or use the Little Foot. This specialty presser foot has an accurate ¼" (6 mm) seam guide and is notched ¼" (6 mm) in front of and behind the center needle position. The notches provide an exact reference for starting, stopping, and pivoting.

Stitching traditional quilt patterns using plaid fabrics is a great way to experiment with the way colors, stripes, and designs work together. And best of all, there's no matching involved!

Plaid Pinwheel

Combine plaid fabric that has a dominant stripe with solid-colored fabric to create a design that seems to spin like a pinwheel!

Gather Supplies

❑ All-purpose thread
❑ Little Foot or other foot with ¼" (6 mm) marking
❑ Rotary cutter and mat
❑ Half-square ruler
❑ Quilting ruler
❑ Fusible interfacing

Create Plaid Pinwheel

1. Cut and join fabric strips.

• Cut each fabric into 2" (5 cm) crosswise strips.

• Decide which plaid to match with each solid and use those pairings throughout.

• Match one plaid strip to one solid strip, right sides together. Stitch along *each* lengthwise edge with ¼" (6 mm) seam allowances *(Diagram A)*.

• Repeat, joining the remaining sets of fabrics.

2. Cut the joined strips into 16 right triangles, using a quilting ruler. For the jumper pinwheel design, I used 4 squares for the center blocks and 12 squares to surround the central blocks.

• Place the tip of the ruler at the top right end of the seamed strips. Align the 45°-angle marking on the ruler with one of the plaid lines, placing it parallel to the opposite lengthwise edge. Cut along the edge of the ruler *(Diagram B)*.

• Flip the ruler over, placing the outer edge of the ruler at the lower right edge of the strip and aligning the 45°-angle marking with a plaid line. Cut along the edge of the ruler. Repeat to cut 16 triangles *(Diagram C)*.

3. Open the right triangles.

• Remove the two or three stitches at the point of the triangle *(Diagram D)*.

• Press the seam toward the solid-colored fabric.

4. Arrange the quilt blocks into the Pinwheel pattern shown in *Diagram E*; stitch them together using the chain-stitching method detailed on page 76.

5. Back the block with fusible interfacing to cover the raw edges.

Making the Plaid Pinwheel

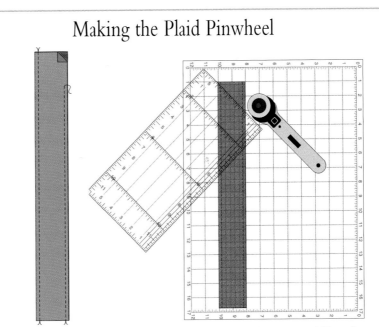

Diagram A: Stitch plaid strip to solid strip.

Diagram B: Cut strip at 45° angle.

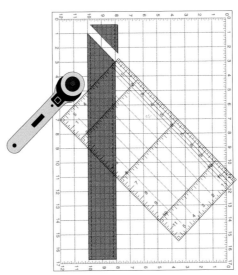

Diagram C: Flip ruler over to cut second 45° angle.

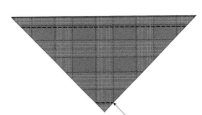

Diagram D: Remove stitches at triangle point.

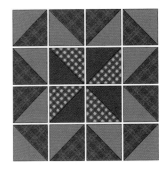

Diagram E: Assemble blocks into Pinwheel pattern.

Wall Hanging Option

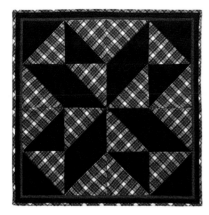

To sew a plaid Pinwheel wall hanging, use the instructions on pages 74 and 75, with the following variations.
• Buy 1 yard (.9 m) each of a plaid and a solid fabric. You'll need additional fabric for the backing, binding, and borders.
• Cut each fabric into four 6½" (16.5 cm) crosswise strips.
• Join one strip of each fabric, right sides together, stitching along both lengthwise edges with ¼" (6 mm) seam allowances.
• Cut strips using rotary cutting as detailed in Step 2 on page 75.
• Arrange blocks into a Pinwheel (photo and *Diagram E* on page 75).
• Add backing, batting, and borders. Quilt and bind as desired.

> *Note from Nancy*
> *My staff quilted the layers using red thread and a zigzag stitch. These stitches add interest to the homespun look of the wall hanging.*

Time-saver

Make more than one Pinwheel block at once. By cutting all the parts at the same time and chain-piecing them, you'll be through in less time than you would need to sew each project separately.

Seminole Plaidwork

Seminole patchwork requires piecing many small fabric scraps to make chevrons. By choosing plaid fabrics for Seminole piecing, you simplify the sewing. Because plaid combines colors and stripes, the chevron effect is built in, so you keep piecing to a minimum.

Select Fabrics

Choose three coordinating plaids: a small, a medium, and a large one.
Select a coordinating solid fabric.

Get Ready

Set up sewing machine or serger as detailed on page 74. See Get Ready for Plaid Pinwheel.

Create Seminole Plaidwork

1. Cut fabric strips. Adjust strip size if desired.
• Cut 3" (7.5 cm) crosswise strips of the three coordinating plaids.
• Cut 2" (5 cm) strips of the coordinating solid fabric *(Diagram A)*.

2. Join the fabric strips.
• Stitch strips together with ¼" (6 mm) seam allowances, alternating plaid and solid strips.
• Continue adding strips until the pieced section is approximately 4" (10 cm) longer than the pattern piece *(Diagram B)*.
• Press seam allowances in one direction.

3. Recut the strips into sections.

> *Note from Nancy*
> *My denim fabric was heavier than my plaid fabrics, so I pressed all the seams toward the plaids (the lighter-weight fabric). The important thing is to be consistent.*

• Fold the plaidwork section in half, right sides together, meeting short ends and aligning plaids.
• Cut the open ends of the folded sections at an angle. Use a 30°, a 45°, or a 60° angle on a cutting mat, depending on personal preference.

• Cut the plaidwork section into 2" (5 cm) strips, using the cut angle as the baseline. Keep pairs of strips together.

4. Seam the pairs.

• Stitch each of the pairs together along one cut edge, right sides together. Chevrons in a flame-stitch pattern will appear on the right side.

• Press seam flat and then press seam to one side *(Diagram D).*

5. Stitch the completed pairs together until the patchwork meets the pattern size.

6. Back the plaidwork with a layer of knit or flannel to cover all the raw edges and make the new fabric softer.

7. Cut out the pattern, using Seminole plaidwork fabric where appropriate, and finish the top according to your pattern guide sheet.

Making Seminole Plaidwork

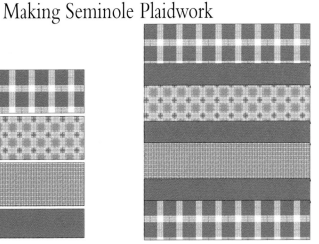

Diagram A: Cut 3" plaid strips and 2" solid strips.

Diagram B: Join strips

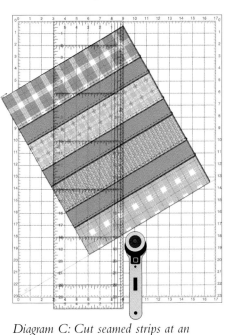

Diagram C: Cut seamed strips at an angle.

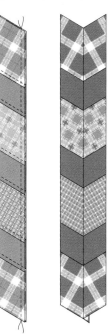

Diagram D: Stitch pairs together.

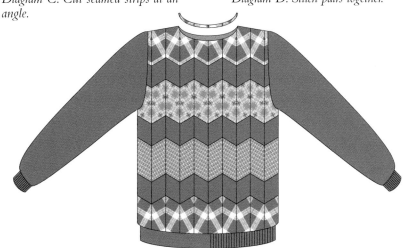

Diagram E: Trim neckline as needed for fit.

Courthouse Steps

This variation of the Courthouse Steps quilt pattern uses two plaids and a solid to create an eye-catching accent that's great fun to sew!

Select Fabrics

Choose two coordinating plaid fabrics.

Select a coordinating solid fabric.

Get Ready

Set up sewing machine or serger as detailed on page 74. See Get Ready for Plaid Pinwheel.

Create Plaid Courthouse Steps

1. Cut each fabric into 1¼" (3.2 cm) crosswise strips.

> *Note from Nancy*
> *I first cut with scissors so that I am sure to follow the plaid line precisely. After the initial cut, I use a rotary cutter and mat to speed cutting.*

2. Create the middle sections. Use ¼" (6 mm) seam allowances throughout. *Chain-piecing techniques are explained on page 72.*

• Use two solid strips and one plaid strip.

• Join one plaid strip and one solid strip right sides together. Using a sewing machine or a serger, stitch one lengthwise edge.

• Open the stitched strip and place the second solid strip so that one lengthwise edge matches the unstitched lengthwise edge of the plaid strip, right sides together. Stitch *(Diagram A)*. These stitched strips are commonly referred to as *strata*.

• Press the seam allowances away from the plaid strip.

• Cut the strata into 1¼" (3.2 cm) middle sections. You must cut sections the same width as the original strips. Cut as many sections as there will be blocks.

3. Stitch or serge a plaid strip on each side of the middle sections, chain-piecing them together.

• Match one of the middle sections to one plaid strip, right sides together with the plaid strip facing up.

• Join the two strips along one lengthwise edge *(Diagram B)*.

• Match a second middle section to the cut edge of the same plaid strip, right sides together, butting it against the first middle section. Continue sewing or serging.

• Repeat until all middle sections have been joined to a plaid strip.

• Repeat, joining another plaid strip to the opposite side of the middle sections, again chain-piecing them together.

• Press seam allowances away from the middle sections, toward the plaid strip.

• Cut the pieced sections apart, following the edge of each middle section as a guide *(Diagram C)*.

4. Add a solid strip to opposite sides of the block.

• Rotate the quilt block a quarter turn. Repeat Step 3 to stitch solid strips to two sides of the quilt block (Diagram D).

• Press the seam allowances toward the outer strips, away from the center. Press the block right side to make sure no tucks form on the top.

• Cut the sections apart, using the length of the quilt block as a guide.

5. Continue adding strips to complete blocks. Finished block size should be approximately 4" (10 cm).

• Rotate the blocks a quarter turn so that the added strips are at the top and the bottom.

• Repeat this process of adding plaid and solid strips until you have added two steps of each color to the center, alternating plaid and solid strips (Diagram E).

6. Complete additional blocks as needed following the same sequence.

7. Arrange the blocks to fit your pattern size. Stitch the blocks together.

Making Courthouse Steps

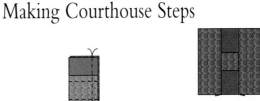

Diag. C: Cut sections apart.

Diag. D: Stitch solid strips to 2 sides of block.

Diagram A: Stitch strips to make strata.

Diagram B: Join middle sections to 1 plaid strip.

Diagram E: Alternate adding plaid and solid strips.

Another Idea

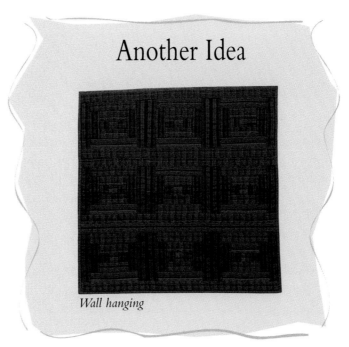

Wall hanging

Heirloom Patchwork

Combine two different art forms—patchwork and heirloom sewing—for sensational embellishments.

Gather Basic Supplies

You need all the general supplies listed below for any Heirloom Patchwork technique. Notions to streamline individual patchwork techniques are listed with each specific technique.

- ❑ Cotton or rayon embroidery thread
- ❑ Press cloth
- ❑ Appliqué scissors
- ❑ Spray starch
- ❑ Water-soluble stabilizer
- ❑ Fabric-marking pen or pencil (non-permanent)
- ❑ Microtex® size 60 or 70 sharp needle
- ❑ See-through ruler

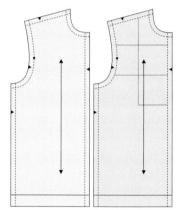

Diagram A: Mark squares on duplicate pattern.

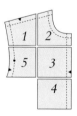

Diagram B: Number pattern pieces.

Instead of cotton strips, I sashed these patchwork blocks using ½" (1.3 cm) entredeux, an heirloom trim. It gives my shirt a delicate, feminine touch.

Plan the Patchwork Design

Take time to plan your design. Preliminary planning gives you a chance to see how the finished project will look before you begin sewing.

1. Select a pattern. Determine where to place the heirloom patchwork and measure the amount of space available for the design.

2. Choose the number, size, and position of blocks. I cut 5" (12.5-cm) squares.

• Trace a duplicate of your pattern so that the original pattern remains intact.

• Outline the squares on the new pattern, drawing vertical lines parallel to the center front and horizontal lines perpendicular to the vertical lines. Not all block sections will be square, since they must conform to the shape of the pattern at the shoulders, armholes, and neckline *(Diagram A)*.

Don't add seam allowances to the block pattern pieces. The entredeux that connects the square adds precisely the amount eliminated by seam allowances.

Make a pattern for each piece of the finished quilt design, indicating heirloom technique you plan to use on each block. Number the pattern pieces for easy reference *(Diagram B)*.

Select Fabrics

Choose 100% cotton batiste or cotton-blend batiste.

Buy 2 to 3 yards (1.6 to 2.4 m) of ½"-wide (1.3 cm-wide) entredeux.

Get Ready

✔ For the Shark's Teeth block, cut crosswise strips 2½ times wider than the finished patchwork block. For example, for a 5" (12.5 cm) finished square, cut a fabric strip 12½" (31.8 cm) wide.

✔ For all other sections, cut crosswise strips of fabric 2" (5 cm) wider than the finished block size.

✔ Stiffen the fabric to give it additional body so that it remains smooth and flat during stitching. Apply several light coats of spray starch or back the fabric with a water-soluble stabilizer.

✔ Insert a Microtex sharp needle. See page 14 for information about sewing machine needles.

✔ Thread the needle and the bobbin with embroidery thread.

✔ Set the sewing machine for a straightstitch.

Crossover Tucks Block

Crossover tucks create an interesting windowpane effect. Basic marking and straightstitching techniques are all that's required.

Gather Supplies

In addition to the basic supplies listed on page 80, you need a blindhem foot.

Get Ready

✔ Replace the conventional foot with the blindhem foot.

✔ Determine how wide each tuck will be. I stitched ⅛" (3 mm) tucks, but you may like a wider or a narrower tuck. Position the blindhem foot's guide that distance from the needle.

Create Crossover Tucks

1. Using the fabric marker, grid the right side of the fabric, marking vertical and horizontal tucks 1½" (3.8 cm) apart *(Diagram A)*.

2. Fold and press the fabric along each marked vertical line, wrong sides together.

3. Align the fabric so that the first tuck's folded edge meets the blindhem foot guide; stitch. Repeat for all remaining vertical tucks *(see photo above right)*.

4. Press all tucks in one direction *(Diagram B)*.

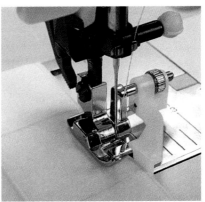

Blindhem foot

5. Press and stitch crosswise tucks. Stitch across the vertical tucks in the same direction as the tucks were pressed.

6. Press tucks in one direction *(Diagram C)*.

7. Fold crossover tucks strip in half. Place pattern piece 1 on strip and cut.

Making Crossover Tucks

1½"

1½"

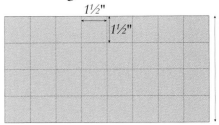

Diagram A: Mark grid on fabric right side.

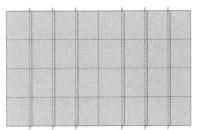

Diagram B: Stitch vertical tucks and press.

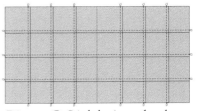

Diagram C: Stitch horizontal tucks; press.

Pleated Patchwork

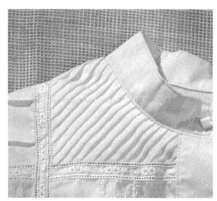

Make rows and rows of uniform pleats. Then use the pleated section as a patchwork element, placing it at any angle you prefer.

Gather Supplies

In addition to the basic supplies listed on page 80, you may want to use Hot Tape®.

Note from Nancy
Hot Tape adhesive-backed tape has markings every ¼" (6 mm). You can press right over the tape when you apply it to fabric since the tape withstands the heat of an iron up to five minutes without leaving residue on the fabric.

Create Pleated Patchwork

Hot Tape Method

1. Place a strip of Hot Tape at each side of the fabric, taking care that the same markings are at the top of each edge.
2. Fold along corresponding lines of the tape. Bring the fold to another set of tape lines, skipping several markings to form a pleat. Press. Repeat across the fabric's length. Hold fabric taut with each fold for best results *(Diagram A)*.
3. Remove the tape after completing all the pleats. Pin along both sides of each pleat after removing the tape to keep the pleats in position.

Traditional Method

1. Fold the fabric strip in half, meeting lengthwise edges.
2. Place a see-through ruler along the lengthwise edge. Cut ¼" (6 mm) nips through both fabric layers at every ¼" (6 mm) marking *(Diagram B)*.
3. Fold the fabric at the first set of nips; press. Meet the pressed pleat to the third set of nips. At the fourth set of nips, repeat the process. Repeat across the fabric width *(Diagram C)*.

4. Fold pleated strip in half. Place pattern piece 2 on fabric and cut.

Note from Nancy
Make these pleats any distance apart that you want. Experiment! You get different effects, depending on the distance between pleats and the depth of individual pleats.

Creating Pleated Patchwork

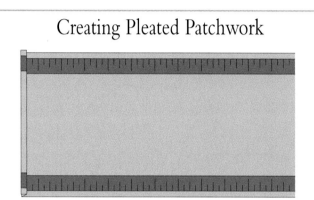

Diagram A: Fold along matching lines of tape.

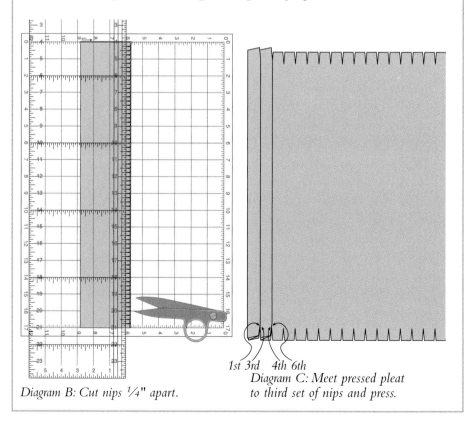

1st 3rd 4th 6th
Diagram B: Cut nips ¼" apart.
Diagram C: Meet pressed pleat to third set of nips and press.

Patchwork with Decorative Stitching

Note from Nancy
Always test decorative stitching on a fabric scrap. If the fabric is very lightweight, you may need to use two layers of stabilizer. Save time and avoid frustration by experimenting before you work on the project.

Sewing a band of decorative stitches down the center of a fabric strip is another attractive embellishment. Select any decorative stitch or a combination of stitches. You're the designer!

Gather Supplies

In addition to basic supplies listed on page 80, you need a machine embroidery foot.

Get Ready

Replace the conventional foot with the embroidery foot.

Create Patchwork with Decorative Stitching

1. Fold the fabric strip in half. Press to mark the center.
2. Back the fabric with water-soluble stabilizer.
3. Stitch along the marked line with one or more decorative stitches *(Diagram)*.
4. Remove the stabilizer and fold the fabric strip in half. Place pattern piece 3 on strip and cut. Be sure to center the pattern on the strip's design.

Time-savers

🕐 Using the same color thread as your fabric for decorative stitching is a classic heirloom technique. However, if you choose a thread just a shade lighter or darker than your fabric, your stitching will stand out more.

🕐 Add decorative stitching to solid-colored flat sheets and pillowcases to make heirloom-quality wedding gifts.

🕐 If your sewing machine doesn't have programmed decorative stitches, mark a simple embroidery design on the fabric.

🕐 For inspiration, look at old linens in second-hand or antiques stores. A discolored napkin may be a great bargain if you can copy its decorative stitching pattern. Trace the design on paper using a light box (or placing the napkin and paper on a glass-topped table with a lamp underneath).

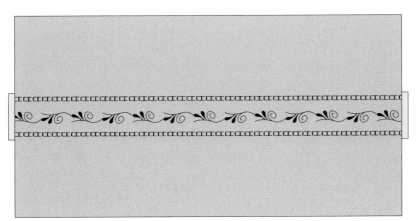

Diagram: Stitch along marked line.

Shark's Teeth Patchwork

Gather Supplies

In addition to basic supplies listed on page 80, you need:

❑ Tuck and Point Guide
❑ Paper-backed fusible web

Note from Nancy
A Tuck and Point Guide makes marking, clipping, and folding points a breeze! This clear plastic ruler is marked for ½" (1.3 cm), ¾" (2 cm), and 1" (2.5 cm) tucks and points.

Get Ready

Use basic setup as detailed in Get Ready on page 81.

Note from Nancy
Remember: cut fabric strips 2½ times wider than the finished block size. Shark's Teeth work best in blocks at least 4½" (11.5 cm) wide.

Create Shark's Teeth Patchwork

1. Mark the strip, drawing lines on the right side of the fabric. Mark first line 1½" (3.8 cm) from the top cut edge. Mark five additional lines 1½" (3.8 cm) apart *(Diagram A)*.

2. Fold and press along each marked line, *wrong* sides together.

3. Stitch ½" (1.3 cm) from all folded edges, forming ½" (1.3 cm) pleats. Press all pleats in one direction *(Diagram B)*.

4. Cut the strip in half, creating two equal-size blocks to mark.

5. Mark the cutting lines for the Shark's Teeth, using a conventional ruler or a Tuck and Point Guide.

• Fold the block in half, meeting ends of tucks. Press to mark the center.

• Open block. Mark the folded edge's center on the first, third, and fifth tucks.

• On the second, fourth, and sixth tucks, measure ½" (1.3 cm) on each side of the center. Mark the folded edge *(two marks)*.

• On the third row, measure and mark the folded edge 1" (2.5 cm) on each side of the center mark *(three marks)*.

• On the fourth row, measure and mark the folded edge 1" (2.5 cm) from the original marks *(four marks)*.

• On the fifth row, measure and mark the folded edge 1" (2.5 cm) and 2" (5 cm) on each side of the center mark *(five marks)*.

• On the sixth row, measure and mark the folded edge 1" (2.5 cm) and 2" (5 cm) on each side of the original marks *(six marks—Diagram C)*.

6. Apply ⅜"-wide (1 cm-wide) strips of paper-backed fusible web within the area where you will form Shark's Teeth.

• On each row, fuse the web to the tuck's underside, beginning ½" (1.3 cm) before the first mark and ending ½" (1.3 cm) after the last mark.

• Remove paper backing from fusible web *(Diagram D)*.

7. Clip from each mark to within a few threads of the stitching line *(Diagram E)*.

8. Form the teeth.

• Fold each side of the clip under to form a point, meeting the cut edge to the stitching line on the wrong side. Finger-press *(Diagram F)*.

• Steam-press. The fusible web holds the teeth in place *(Diagram G)*.

Note from Nancy
Do not try to make this block in a hurry! Take your time folding and pressing the points so that your finished Shark's Teeth will be sharp and accurate.

9. Secure the Shark's Teeth with a very narrow zigzag stitch.

• Use thread matched to the fabric.

• With right side up, zigzag along each tuck stitching line. One edge of the stitch should just touch the stitching line, while the other edge stitches into the cut edges to hold them in place. The stitching goes only through the *teeth*, not through the fabric under the teeth *(Diagram H)*.

10. Center pattern piece 4 on each block and cut to finished size.

Creating Shark's Teeth Patchwork

Diagram A: Mark fold lines.

Diagram B: Stitch ½" from folded edge.

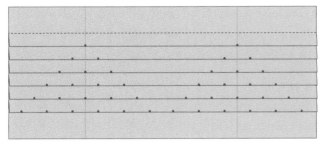

Diagram C: Mark cutting lines.

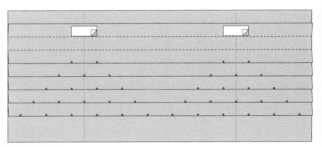

Diagram D: Fuse web to underside of tuck and remove backing.

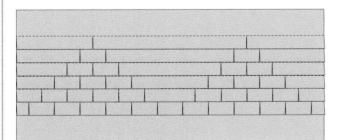

Diagram E: Clip each "tooth."

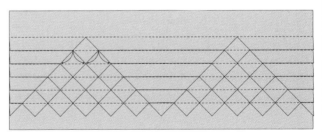

Diagram F: Fold each side of clip under to form point.

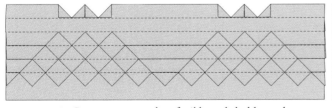

Diagram G: Steam-press so that fusible web holds teeth.

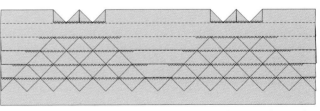

Diagram H: Zigzag through teeth only, not fabric underneath.

Pintuck Patchwork

Rows and rows of delicate pintucks accent this heirloom patchwork. The secret to successful pintucks is using a double needle and a pintuck foot.

Gather Supplies

In addition to the basic supplies listed on page 80, you need:
- ❑ 1.6/80 or 2.0/80 double needle
- ❑ Pintuck foot (5- or 7-groove foot)
- ❑ Cording blade (optional)
- ❑ Two spools cotton or rayon thread

Get Ready

- ✔ Replace your conventional machine needle with the double needle.
- ✔ Replace the conventional presser foot with the pintuck foot.
- ✔ Attach the cording blade if desired.
- ✔ Slightly tighten the upper tension to make the fabric tuck.
- ✔ Thread the double needle and the bobbin with embroidery thread.

Note from Nancy

When threading the machine, save time and avoid trouble by treating the two threads as one until you reach the double needle. When you thread both through the same side of the tension disk, each thread receives the same tension, and your stitching is uniform and balanced.

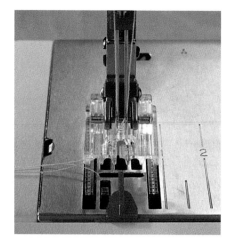

Double needle, pintuck foot, and cording blade

Create Pintucks

1. Pull a thread near one edge of the fabric strip to provide a line for guiding the first row of stitching. Or draw a line along the straight of grain to serve as a stitching guide.

2. Stitch the first pintuck, following the marked line. This line of stitching is critical, since it establishes the position for subsequent rows of stitching. If this row is straight, others are likely to be straight, too *(Diagram A)*.

3. Align the first pintuck in one of the grooves of the pintuck foot. The groove select determines the distance between the pintuck rows. Stitch all remaining rows in the same manner, guiding the previous row in the groove *(Diagram B)*.

4. Fold the pintuck strip in half. Place pattern piece 5 on the strip and cut *(Diagram C)*.

Creating Pintucks

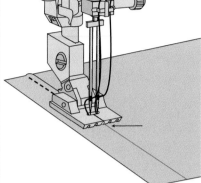

Diagram A: Stitch first pintuck, following marked line.

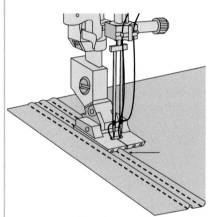

Diagram B: Align first pintuck in groove of foot and stitch.

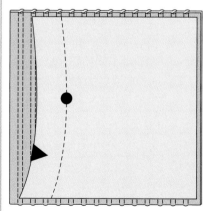

Diagram C: Fold pintuck patchwork in half and cut pattern piece.

Assemble the Quilt Blocks

Now it's time to join the various quilt blocks. Use all five of the techniques or a combination of two or three. The choice is yours!

I used bands of ½"-wide (1.3 cm-wide) entredeux to join my blocks. The entredeux includes ¼" (6 mm) seam allowances on each side of the trim, making application simple.

1. Cut all heirloom blocks to the size of the original pattern. Remember, some of the blocks near the shoulder, neckline, and armhole will be irregularly shaped rather than square *(Diagram A)*.

2. Join blocks into vertical strips.

• Cut entredeux the same length as the blocks it will connect. Spray starch the trim; press.

• Straightstitch the entredeux to the quilt block, right sides together, using a medium stitch length and sewing next to the well of the entredeux *(Diagram B)*.

• Press seam allowances away from the entredeux, toward the blouse.

• Set the sewing machine for a medium width and length zigzag. Working from the strip right side, zigzag the seam flat. One edge of the zigzag should fall in the quilt block and the other edge in the hole of the entredeux *(Diagram C)*.

• Flip the block to the wrong side and trim away the excess seam allowances close to the stitching.

• Add a strip of entredeux at the lower edge of each vertical strip.

3. Join the vertical blocks with another length of entredeux, using the technique detailed above.

Note from Nancy
Appliqué scissors simplify this process by letting you trim closely without cutting the fashion fabric. Place the bill of the scissors under the fabric you want to trim, and cut. It's easy!

Appliqué scissors

Assembling Heirloom Patchwork

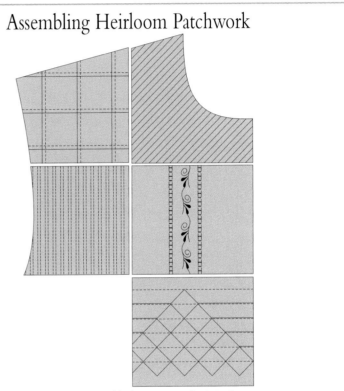

Diagram A: Cut blocks to size of original pattern.

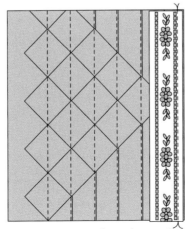

Diagram B: Straightstitch entredeux.

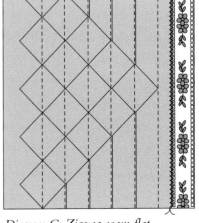

Diagram C: Zigzag seam flat.

4. Stitch the patchwork section to the garment fabric.

• Trim the remaining entredeux seam allowance close to the embroidery.

• Overlap the quilted section on the blouse fabric; pin.

• Cut the blouse front according to the original pattern and trim the excess after adding the embellished section. Or when you cut out the front, reduce the amount of fabric required by eliminating the parts of the blouse that will be covered with quilt blocks, allowing room to overlap the section.

• Zigzag along the entredeux, with one part of the zigzag falling in the hole of the entredeux and the other part in the fabric *(Diagram G)*.

• On the wrong side of the garment, trim the garment fabric behind the embellished sections, leaving a ¼" (6 mm) seam allowance *(Diagram H)*.

• Press the seam away from the entredeux. Zigzag again to reinforce and hold the seam allowance in place.

• Trim excess seam allowances that extend beyond the zigzagging *(Diagram I)*.

5. Complete the garment following your pattern guide sheet.

Attaching Heirloom Patchwork to a Garment

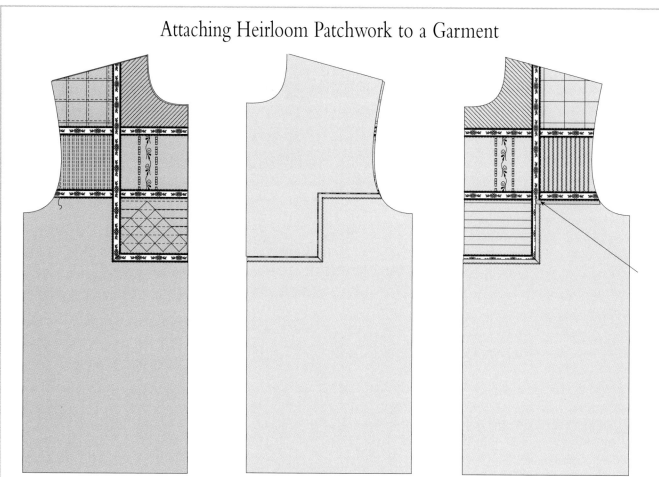

Diagram G: Zigzag entredeux to blouse fabric.

Diagram H: Trim garment fabric from behind embellished blocks.

Diagram I: Trim excess seam allowances beyond zigzagging.

More Ideas

Baptism dress

Bonnet

Pillow

Shirt

Lingerie

Ribbing Patchwork

This technique provides an easy way to turn a basic T-shirt into a Wow! shirt.

3. Stitch the main color band to one end of the pieced strip *(Diagram A)*.
4. Measure the length of the new band. Trim to correct size by removing the excess fabric from the main color.
5. Determine placement for the ribbing patchwork. Attach the band to the neckline, following the pattern guide sheet instructions.
6. Topstitch around the neckline using the stretch double needle, stitching with the right needle next to the seam and the left needle on the garment *(Diagram B)*.

Note from Nancy
The blue bar at the top of stretch double needles distinguishes them from conventional double needles, which have a red bar.

Gather Supplies
❏ Size 90 stretch needle
❏ 4.0 mm stretch double needle

Select Fabrics
For the primary neckline band fabric, choose ribbing to match the main garment fabric.

For patchwork pieces, select at least two colors of ribbing that coordinate or contrast with the neckline band fabric. Use woven or nonwoven fabric.

Get Ready
✔ Insert the stretch needle in the machine.
✔ Use thread in the needle and the bobbin that matches the fabric.
✔ Set the sewing machine for a straightstitch.

Note from Nancy
Use a striped fabric as inspiration for ribbing patchwork. Notice the colors and the sizes of the stripes and consider adapting those combinations.

Create Ribbing Patchwork
1. Cut ribbing in various sizes, keeping the width the same as the main neckline band fabric. Add ½" (1.3 cm) to each accent fabric for seam allowances.
2. Join the accent pieces with a ¼" (6 mm) seam allowance. Finger-press the seams open. (Pressing with an iron could flatten and remove the stretch from the band.)

Diagram A: Stitch main color band to pieced strip.

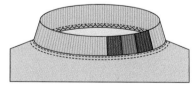

Diagram B: Topstitch around neckline.

Create Horizontal Ribbing Patchwork

1. Cut your ribbing strips ¾" to 1½" (2 cm to 3.8 cm) wide, each the length of your garment opening. Use the matching color for the underside of the band. The total width should be the same as if the ribbing was cut from one fabric, plus seam allowances.

2. Join the strips with ¼" (6 mm) seam allowances, being careful not to stretch the fabrics. Using a narrow zigzag stitch helps build in stretch *(Diagram C)*.

3. Finger-press the seams. Join the narrow ends of the stitched strips, staggering the seam allowances to reduce bulk *(Diagram D)*.

4. Attach the band to the neckline, sleeve, or waistband, following the pattern guide sheet instructions.

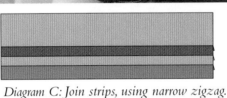

Diagram C: Join strips, using narrow zigzag.

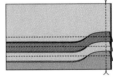

Diagram D: Join strips, staggering seam allowances

Create Woven Fabric Ribbing Patchwork

The neckline of a casual shirt is the perfect place to showcase a leftover patchwork piece. I used a strip of the same leftover patchwork in the pocket of the shirt. You could use a piece of printed woven fabric instead of patchwork, matching pants or a skirt you plan to wear with the blouse.

• Insert a 3" (7.5 cm) or smaller section of woven fabric into the neckline, using the guidelines detailed above. The non-stretch section is small enough that it won't keep the neckline from stretching.

Note from Nancy
If your insert is larger than 3" (7.5 cm), consider trimming the neckline slightly larger before you add the band to ensure that the garment slips easily over your head.

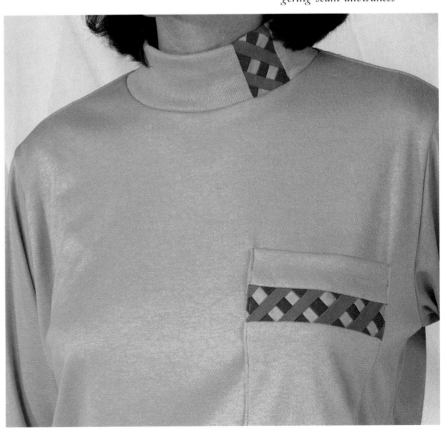

Interweave bias strips to create Bias Surface Texture *(left and page 100)*. Couch decorative threads onto a blouse, and then weave in more threads for Couched Weaving *(right and page 115)*. ▶

My easy techniques to create dimension and texture on fabric allow you to become your own fabric designer.

Textured Embellishments

◀ Weave ribbons with fabric strips to create Dimensional Weaving *(left and page 108)*. Use silk ribbon in the bobbin to create luxurious Silk-Ribbon Bobbin Texture on a jacket lapel. *(right and page 99)*. ▶

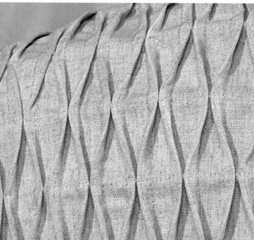

◀ Stitch straight tucks into flat fabric, and stitch horizontally across them to create distinctive Diamond Tucks on a jacket *(left and page 94)*.

Open-Weave Vest,
page 106

Diamond Tucks

They say diamonds are a girl's best friend, and these diamonds will add a special sparkle to your next garment!

Simple straightstitching and some pressing are all you do to create these unusual tucks. Making the tucks takes a little time, but you will be pleased with the results.

Gather Supplies
❑ All-purpose thread that matches the fabric
❑ Size 80 or 90 universal needle
❑ Straight-edge ruler
❑ Temporary fabric marker or chalk
❑ Rotary-cutting mat

Select Fabric
Choose fashion fabric, avoiding prints. See your pattern for the amount. Allow about ½ yard (46 cm) extra fabric for making tucks.

Get Ready
✔ Thread the needle and the bobbin with all-purpose thread.
✔ Adjust the machine for a slightly longer-than-normal straightstitch, approximately 10 stitches per inch.

Create Diamond Tucks
1. Cut a rectangle of fabric that is two times the width and 2" (5 cm) longer than the pattern piece that will feature the diamond tucks.
2. Using the straight-edge ruler and a marker or chalk, draw vertical lines 1" (2.5 cm) apart on the right side of the fabric *(Diagram A)*. These marks must be removed later, so use a marker that you can easily remove from the fabric.

Note from Nancy
For more accuracy, place the fabric on a gridded surface such as a rotary-cutting mat. Use the lines on the mat as the measuring tool by aligning the ruler with the gridded markings at the top and bottom of the mat to mark (Diagram B).

3. Fold the fabric along the first marked line, wrong sides together; press. Refold along the second marked line; press along the fold. Press only the fold, so that you don't remove the previously pressed fold *(Diagram C)*. Repeat until all the folds are pressed along the marked lines *(Diagram D)*.
4. Stitch vertical tucks ¼" (6 mm) from each fold line, wrong sides together *(Diagram E)*. Tips for stitching a consistent ¼" seam are on page 74.

5. Press all tucks in one direction.
6. Using a marker or chalk, draw horizontal lines every 1½" or 3.8 cm *(Diagram F)*. Remember, these dimensions are only guidelines, not hard-and-fast rules. Adjust measurements as desired.
7. Stitch horizontal lines as follows:
• **Row 1**: Meet folded edges of the first two vertical tucks; pin. Meet folded edges of the third and fourth tucks; pin. Continue meeting folded edges and pinning along the entire horizontal line. Stitch through the tucks, following the horizontal marking *(Diagram G)*.
• **Row 2:** Fold the first tuck toward the cut edge of the fabric; pin. Meet the edges of the second and third tucks; pin. Meet edges of the fourth and fifth tucks; pin. Continue meeting folded edges and pinning along

second horizontal line. Stitch through the tucks, following the horizontal marking. The two stitched rows will begin to form a diamond pattern (Diagram H).

Continue folding, pinning, and stitching along each horizontal line, alternating Row 1 and Row 2, until you have stitched all horizontal rows (Diagram I).

Creating Diamond Tucks

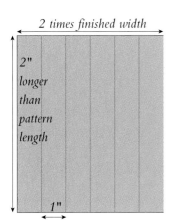

Diagram A: Draw vertical lines on fabric.

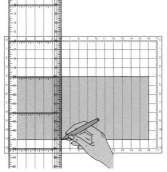

Diagram B: Place fabric on gridded surface to mark.

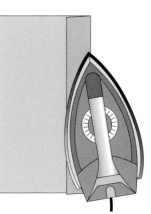

Diagram C: Press along fold.

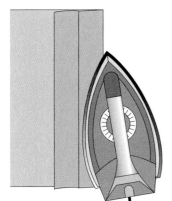

Diagram D: Press other folds, being careful not to remove previously pressed folds.

Diagram E: Stitch vertical tuck ¼" from fold line.

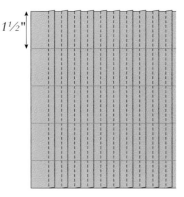

Diagram F: Draw horizontal lines every 1½".

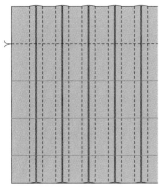

Diagram G: Meet folded edges and stitch along a horizontal line.

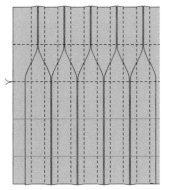

Diagram H: Diamond pattern begins to form when stitching second line.

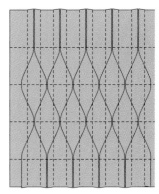

Diagram I: Continue to stitch all horizontal lines.

Serged Diamond Tucks

Gather Supplies

In addition to the basic supplies for Diamond Tucks, you need:
❑ All-purpose serger thread
❑ Decorative serger thread in two coordinating or contrasting colors

Get Ready

✔ Adjust the serger for a 3-thread overlock stitch.
✔ Use only the left needle.
✔ Thread the left needle with all-purpose serger thread.
✔ Thread the upper and lower loopers with decorative threads of two different colors.
✔ Adjust the stitch width to exactly ¼" (6 mm).
✔ Set the stitch length for a long stitch.
✔ Slightly loosen the upper and lower looper tensions to -1 or -2.

Note from Nancy

You probably need to loosen the tensions on your machine when using decorative threads. Adjustments vary from machine to machine and with different thread and fabric combinations. Always test stitching on a fabric scrap before sewing on your garment.

Create Serged Diamond Tucks

1. Follow steps 1 through 3 on page 94 for Diamond Tucks.
2. Serge along each folded edge, serging from top to bottom on the first row *(Diagram A)*.

Note from Nancy

If possible, raise the serger upper blade when serging along a fold to prevent cutting the fabric. If you can't raise the blade, guide the fabric fold near the blade.

3. Flip the fabric and serge in the opposite direction, (in effect, from bottom to top), on the second row *(Diagram B)*.
4. Repeat, alternating stitching direction on each row to create an interesting two-color effect when the twists are stitched.
5. Mark and stitch the horizontal rows with a conventional sewing machine, using matching thread. Follow the instructions given on page 94.

Serging Diamond Tucks

Diagram A: Serge along the folded edge.

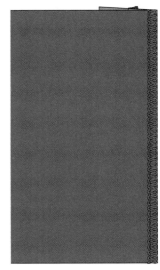

Diagram B: Flip the fabric; serge in the opposite direction.

Bobbin Texture

Sew on the wrong side of fabric to embellish the right side.

Put decorative thread in the bobbin and turn your project wrong side up. Use a straightstitch or a simple decorative stitch for exciting results.

Gather Supplies

❏ All-purpose sewing machine thread
❏ Decorative thread such as Glamour Thread, Pearl Crown Rayon, or ribbon floss
❏ Size 80 or 90 universal needle
❏ Iron-on stabilizer

Select Fabrics

Choose a fashion fabric; see your pattern for amount.

Get Ready

✔ Thread the top of the machine with all-purpose thread that matches the decorative thread.

✔ Set the machine for a straightstitch or an airy decorative stitch. Slightly lengthen the stitch length.
✔ Wind the decorative thread or yarn onto the bobbin by hand.

Note from Nancy

Winding bobbins manually produces less tension in the bobbin thread, so you see more of the thread or yarn on the finished project. Since a bobbin doesn't hold large yardages of these heavier threads, wind several bobbins before you begin to stitch.

✔ Loosen the bobbin tension by turning the tension screw to the left. (Remember, right is tight and left is loose.) Don't turn the screw too far. Make only small adjustments at a time—a quarter turn or less.

Note from Nancy

Don't hesitate to change your bobbin tension! It isn't difficult, provided you take one precaution: Mark the position for normal tension on the bobbin case before making any changes. Use fingernail polish to mark the groove on the tension screw, and place a corresponding mark on the bobbin case. Then you can easily return to the normal setting after you finish decorative stitching.

Marking bobbin tension

✔ Or bypass the tension. Find the large side opening on the bobbin case. Insert the bobbin in the case, and guide the thread out the side opening rather than passing the yarn or thread through the tension slot. Without tension on the bobbin yarn or thread, stitching has a less structured look.

Bypassing bobbin tension

Create Bobbin Texture

1. Trace or transfer the design to the dull side of the stabilizer. Iron the stabilizer onto the wrong side of the fabric *(Diagram A)*.

2. Make a test sample, using the same fabric and stabilizer. Stitch with the wrong side of the sample facing up. Be sure you like the stitching. If not, adjust the bobbin tension, the stitch length, or both.

3. On the project, stitch from the wrong side, following the marked design *(Diagram B)*. Stopping with the needle down makes it easier to turn corners. If desired, fill in portions of the design. Begin by outlining the design, then fill in areas, working from the outside in *(Diagram C)*.

4. If you loosened the tension screw, return it to its original position after completing the decorative stitching.

5. Carefully remove the stabilizer.

Time-saver

Don't throw away your samples! If you like the sample stitching, use it to cover buttons for this project or another.

Making Bobbin Texture

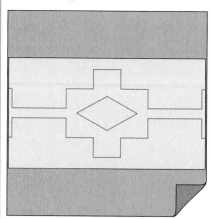

Diagram A: Trace design onto stabilizer, and iron it onto wrong side of fabric.

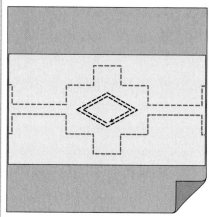

Diagram B: Stitch from wrong side, following design.

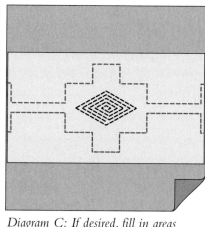

Diagram C: If desired, fill in areas inside design.

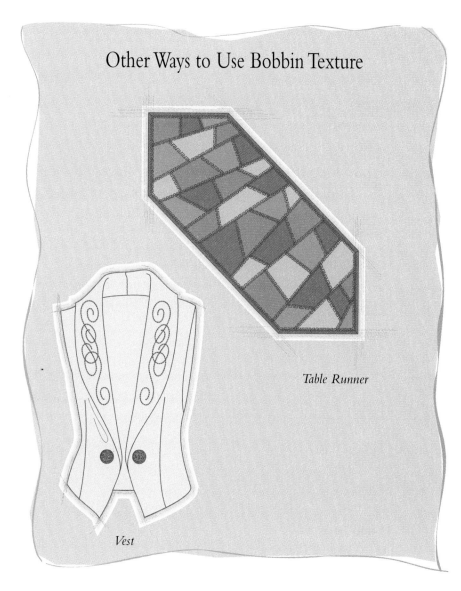

Other Ways to Use Bobbin Texture

Table Runner

Vest

Silk-Ribbon Bobbin Texture

Silk ribbon is another excellent candidate for embellishing from the bobbin. Combine Silk-Ribbon Bobbin Texture with patchwork for a result that resembles something our grandmothers might have stitched by hand on their crazy-pieced quilts.

Gather Supplies

❏ All-purpose sewing machine thread
❏ Size 80 or 90 universal needle
❏ 2 mm silk ribbon in assorted colors

Select Fabrics

Select assorted fabric scraps for the patchwork section.

Choose a fabric for the main project; see your pattern for amount.

Get Ready

✔ Set the sewing machine for a straightstitch, using matching thread in the needle and bobbin.

Create Silk-Ribbon Bobbin Texture

1. Stitch fabric sections together in a crazy-quilting manner. (See Crazy Patchwork on page 68.)
2. Press all seam allowances in one direction. These pressed seams act as a stabilizer for the decorative stitching *(Diagram A)*.
3. Follow the instructions under Get Ready for Bobbin Texture (page 97) to adjust your machine and thread silk ribbon in the bobbin. Choose to

Making Silk-Ribbon Bobbin Texture

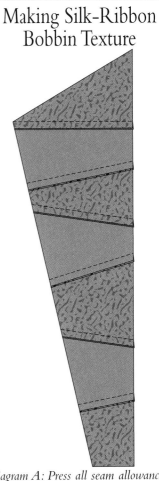

Diagram A: Press all seam allowances in one direction.

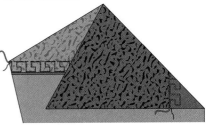

Diagram B: From wrong side, stitch in seam allowance.

bypass, rather than loosen, the bobbin tension. Select an airy decorative stitch.
4. Working from the wrong side of the fabric, stitch in the seam allowance area close to the original stitching line. *(Diagram B)*.
5. Select different decorative stitches and change colors of silk ribbon as desired.

Bias Surface Texture

Add interesting dimension to your next creative project by interweaving bias strips.
These accents can enhance outer edges or add attractive inside detail.

Gather Supplies
- ❑ All-purpose sewing thread
- ❑ Rotary cutter, ruler, and mat
- ❑ Bias tape maker (optional)
- ❑ Tracing paper
- ❑ Liquid fusible web
- ❑ Press cloth

Select Fabric
For easy shaping, choose a light- to medium-weight fabric to use as the bias trim. If the fabric is too heavy, the completed bias may buckle and ripple.

Get Ready
- ✔ Thread the needle and the bobbin with all-purpose thread that matches the fabric.
- ✔ Adjust the machine for a straight-stitch.

Create Bias Surface Texture
1. Cut and join bias strips.
- Cut bias strips 1¾" to 2" (4.5 cm to 5 cm). The strip width depends on the fabric; with thicker fabrics, cut narrower strips. You need two long strips to do the weaving. Cut enough bias strips to go around the edge of your project twice.

Note from Nancy
A Strip Ticket takes the guesswork out of making bias tape in different widths and lengths. A glance at this notion tells you exactly how much fabric you need to make any size bias strip. Calculations include 1" to 7" widths, and 50" to 591" lengths. (Measurements are given in inches.)

- Meet the short ends of two strips, right sides together, offsetting the ends by ¼" or 6 mm *(Diagram A)*. Stitch, using a ¼" (6mm) seam. Press the seam open and trim the triangular ends. Repeat to make two long strips.

2. Create the bias trim.
- Insert the end of one of the bias strips into the wide end of a 1" (25 mm) bias tape maker. Using a straight pin, advance the strip through the tape maker. When the bias strip comes out the narrow end of the tape maker, the outer edges are folded to the center. Press with the tip of the iron.

Bias tape maker

- Continue advancing and pressing the strip through the bias tape maker until the entire length of the bias is pressed.
- Fold the strip again, meeting the folded edges. Press.
- Straightstitch along the folded edges *(Diagram B)*.

Note from Nancy
To make bias tape without a bias tape maker, press both long edges of the bias to the middle of the strip. Fold the strip, meeting the folded edges. Press. Straightstitch along the folded edges.

3. Shape the bias trim.

• Choose a simple, subtle design. Trace the design on paper. The design I used is on page 142.

• Arrange the two bias strips to conform to the design.

• Fuse the strips together at the intersection by placing a drop of liquid fusible web between the strips *(Diagram C)*. Cover the strips with a press cloth and press.

> ### Note from Nancy
> *Liqui Fuse Liquid Fusible Web is like fusible web in a bottle. The nice thing about using it is that you can place the fusible liquid exactly where you want it. Adjust the shape of the bias trim until you are happy with the placement, and then fuse the layers with your iron.*

4. Shape and stitch the bias trim to conform to the project.

• Pin the trim to the fabric.

• Topstitch around the edges to hold the trim in place, pivoting at the intersection points. The scallops create an interesting open weave around the garment edges *(Diagram D)*.

Time-savers

If you don't have liquid fusible web on hand (Step 3), use a glue stick or white household glue. Household glue will wash out, but your topstitching will hold the trim in place.

Use purchased bias tape in a color that contrasts with a purchased vest for a quick project. Use the instructions starting with the last part of Step 2. (Straightstitch along the folded edges.)

Stitching Bias Surface Texture

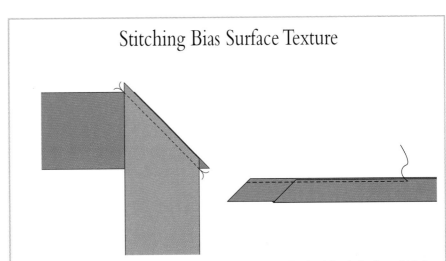

Diagram A: Stitch two strips together.

Diagram B: Straightstitch along folded edges.

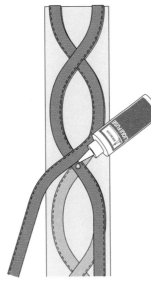

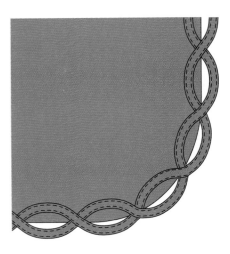

Diagram C: Place liquid fusible web between strips.

Diagram D: Topstitch around edges to hold trim in place.

Celtic Surface Texture

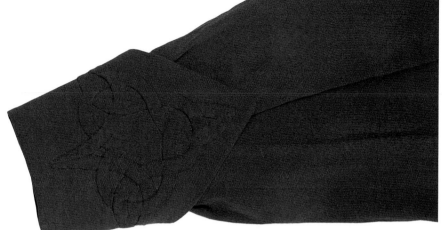

Note from Nancy
You can choose from an interesting assortment of tube turners, ranging in design and price. Many readers ask, "Which turner is the best to buy?" Pictured are three of my favorites: The Narrow Loop Turner (A) turns only tubes and is easy to use. The Collar Point & Tube Turner (B) turns both tubes and corners. The Fasturn (C) turns tubes.

Gather Supplies

❑ All-purpose thread to match fabric
❑ Universal needle
❑ Rotary cutter, ruler, and mat
❑ Tube turner
❑ Celtic Bias Bars
❑ Lightweight fusible interfacing
❑ Paper or plastic template sheet
❑ Fabric marking pencil
❑ Liquid fusible web (optional)
❑ Press cloth (optional)
❑ Monofilament thread
❑ Lingerie/bobbin thread
❑ Embroidery or open toe foot

Select Fabrics

Choose light- to medium-weight fabric with an even stretch on the bias.

Get Ready

✔ Thread the needle and bobbin with thread to match the fashion fabric.
✔ Use the conventional presser foot and a universal needle.
✔ Adjust the machine for a straightstitch.

Create Celtic Surface Texture

1. Make bias strips:
• Cut bias strips 1½" (3.8 cm) wide using rotary cutter, ruler, and mat. Do not join the bias strips; the seams are too bulky to use in this technique.
• Stitch long edges of strips, right sides together, using a narrow ⅛" (3 mm) seam.
• Turn the bias strips right side out using a tube turner.
• Insert a flexible Celtic Bias Bar into the bias tube strip, keeping the seam in the center back of the strip. Steam-press on both sides for super-sharp creases. Push bar through until the entire tube is pressed. Repeat until all tubes are pressed. Be careful because the metal celtic bars become very hot!
2. Press fusible interfacing to the wrong side of the garment piece to be embellished.
3. Trace your design on paper or a plastic template sheet. (The design I used is on page 134.) Cut out the design. Place the template on the fabric and trace around the design with a marker *(Diagram A)*.
4. Pin the bias strips over the design.
• Working on a padded pressing surface, place the end of a bias strip at an intersection, where two strips cross. Pin or use liquid fusible web to keep the strips in place *(Diagram B)*.
• At intersections, weave over or under as needed to secure bias strip. Your design will indicate where to weave the bias strips *(Diagram C)*.
• If the design has points or corners, miter the bias strip by placing the strip to the corner, turning the strip back on itself, and hand-stitching diagonally across the seam *(Diagram D)*. Trim excess bias strip to remove bulk *(Diagram E)*.
• Continue placing bias strips on the design *(Diagram F)*. If you need more than one bias strip to complete the design, butt the ends of the strips together under an intersection *(Diagram G)*.
• If using a liquid fusible web, place a press cloth over the design and fuse the strips into place.
5. Set the machine for stitching the Celtic design to the garment.
• Thread the needle with monofilament thread and the bobbin with

lingerie/bobbin thread.

• Attach an open toe or an embroidery foot.

• Adjust the machine for a blindhem stitch and a stitch width and length of 1.

• Loosen the tension by two notches (for example, from 5 to 3).

6. Stitch around the edges of the design.

• Stitch in a clockwise direction, with the straightstitching beside the bias strips and the zigzag of the blindhem stitch catching the strip. Complete one side at a time *(Diagram H)*.

• At an intersection, one strip is an "over" strip and the other is an "under" strip. When stitching the under strip and approaching the intersection, shorten the stitch length to 0. Sew several stitches in place to anchor the thread. Lift the presser foot and needle over the intersection. Anchor stitch again on the other side of the intersection. Return the stitch length to the original setting and continue stitching. Repeat at each intersection *(Diagram I)*.

• When stitching an over strip, stitch across the intersection *(Diagram J)*.

• Clip threads that cross the bias strips at the intersections.

Bias Surface Texture

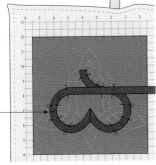

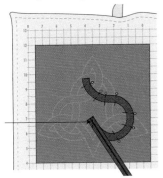

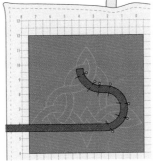

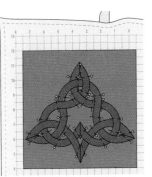

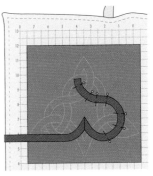

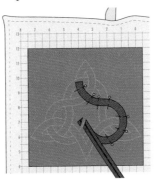

Diagram A: Use a template to trace your design onto fabric.

Diagram B: Pin or fuse strips in place.

Diagram C: Weave over or under as your design indicates.

Diagram D: Miter each corner and hand-stitch in place.

Diagram E: Trim excess bias strip.

Diagram F: Continue placing bias strips on design.

Diagram G: To add new bias strips, butt ends together.

Diagram H: Use a blindhem stitch to sew around edges.

Diagram I: Carry thread over intersections for "under" strips.

Diagram J: Stitch across intersections for "over" strips.

Decorative Weaving

*Transform bits and pieces of fabric, thread, ribbon,
and yarn into an interesting and attractive new fabric.*

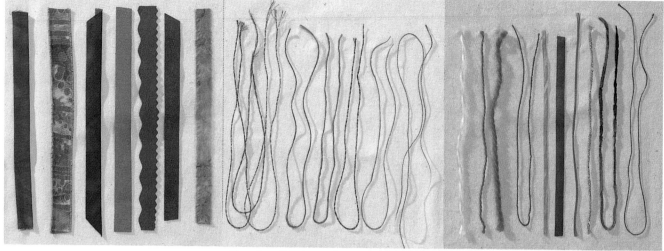

Select one or more of these materials as weaving elements. The strip widths are totally up to the designer—you!

• **Torn fabric strips** (from single layers of fabric) for a homespun look.

• **Leather or Ultrasuede strips**, cut using a rotary cutter, pinking shears, or specialty rotary-cutting blades, such as the wave blade.

• **Bias strips**, especially those made from plaid or checked fabric. (See Folk Art Appliqué on page 48.)

• **Serged strips** (from single layers of fabric) finished with a 3-thread over-lock stitch or rolled-edge stitch for a ribbonlike appearance.

• **Fabric tubes**, narrow or wide, to add dimension. (See Bias Surface Texture on page 100.)

• **Decorative serger thread**, used for the lengthwise threads of a weaving project. (See page 14.)

• **Embroidery floss**, in cotton or silk.

• **Ribbons**, narrow or wide.

• **Yarn**, either decorative or traditional knitting yarns, used for the lengthwise portion of a woven piece.

Strip Weaving

Strip weaving with an even-weave design is an ideal first weaving project. Whatever type strips you choose, the steps are the same. Weaving on a fusible interfacing base streamlines the process by keeping the strips from raveling and stabilizing the fabric.

Gather Basic Supplies

☐ Lightweight fusible interfacing
☐ Padded pressing surface
☐ Press cloth

Select Weaving Elements

Choose one type of fabric strip: torn, leather, bias, serged, or tube.

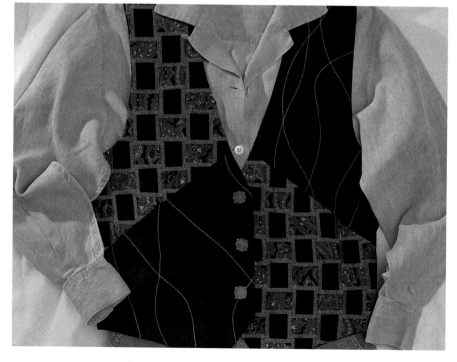

Create Strip Weaving

1. Cut a piece of lightweight fusible interfacing slightly larger than the pattern.

2. Place the interfacing on a padded pressing surface, fusible side up. Place lengthwise strips over the interfacing. Pin along the upper edge *(Diagram A)*.

Note from Nancy
Working on a gridded pressing surface, such as the Pin-Weave Express™ Board, helps you keep the strips parallel during weaving. The padded surface makes it easy to secure strips and weave them in and out.

3. Weave a crosswise strip, alternately threading the strip under and over the lengthwise strips *(Diagram B)*.

4. Add a second crosswise strip *(Diagram C)*, weaving in the opposite order (over-and-under the lengthwise strips). The over and under weaving process creates an even-weave design.

5. After weaving several crosswise strips, cover the woven section with a press cloth and fuse, keeping the strips straight *(Diagram D)*.

6. Repeat until you weave all crosswise strips through the lengthwise strips.

7. **Option:** Speed-weave the crosswise strips.

• Position the lengthwise strips as detailed above.

• Stack half the crosswise strips; weave the stack through the lengthwise strips as if they were a single strip *(Diagram E)*.

• Separate the strips, allowing space between them *(Diagram F)*

• Fill in the spaces between strips with single strips woven in the opposite order.

Strip Weaving

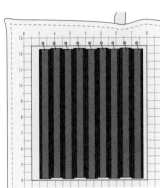

Diagram A: Pin lengthwise strips to a padded surface.

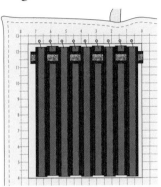

Diagram B: Weave a crosswise strip under and over.

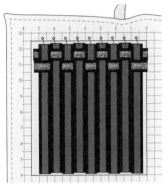

Diagram C: Add a second crosswise strip.

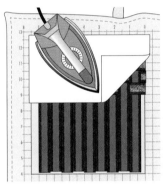

Diagram D: Cover with a press cloth and fuse.

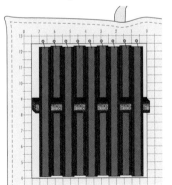

Diagram E: Speed-weave a stack of crosswise strips.

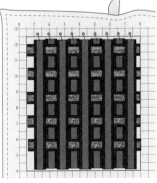

Diagram F: Separate stack, leaving room to weave strips in opposite direction.

Open Weaving

Gather Supplies

In addition to basic weaving supplies, you need:

❑ All-purpose thread to match fabric
❑ Fusible thread
❑ Tissue paper
❑ Tracing paper and tracing wheel
❑ Fusible web (optional)
❑ Machine embroidery thread
❑ Bias tape maker (optional)

Select Weaving Elements

Use a type of fabric strip for weaving: torn, leather, bias, serged, or tube (see page 104). I used 1" (2.5 cm) tube strips to weave the blue vest.

Get Ready

✔ Thread needle and bobbin of the sewing machine with thread that matches the fabric strips.
✔ Adjust the machine for a straight-stitch.
✔ Wind a second bobbin with fusible thread.

Note from Nancy

To create tubes quickly, my staff and I used a Fasturn. To use this handy notion, cut strips of fabric twice your finished tube width plus seam allowances. (For our 1"-wide (2.5 cm-wide) finished tubes, we cut 2½"-wide (6.3 cm-wide) fabric strips.) With right sides together, stitch the lengthwise edges and one short edge with a ¼" (6 mm) seam. To turn the tubes right side out, slip the tube over the Fasturn cylinder, and insert the pigtail wire into the cylinder from the handle end. Turn the hook clockwise, pulling the tail through the fabric. Finally, gently pull the wire back through the cylinder, turning the tube right side out. (Diagram below).

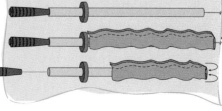

Create Open Weaving

1. Prepare a pattern to serve as the base for weaving.

• If creating a vest, trim away the neck, armhole, and hem seam allowances on the pattern *(Diagram A)*.

• Trace onto tissue paper the pattern piece or pattern section that will include the weaving section. If both sides of the garment will include weaving, stack two sheets of paper. Cut out the tissue paper.

• Grid the tissue paper *(Diagram B)*.

• To create an open look, make certain the grid is larger than the finished width of the weaving strips. If applicable, transfer the grid to the second pattern piece using tracing paper and tracing wheel to ensure that the second piece is a mirror image of the first. I used a 1½" (3.8 cm) grid for the green vest.

2. Weave the fabric tubes, following the gridded pattern.

• Place the lengthwise fabric tubes along one edge of the lengthwise grid. Pin strips to the paper *(Diagram C)*.

• Weave the crosswise strips in and out of the lengthwise strips, again matching one edge of the weave to the grid. Pin ends of the strips to the paper *(Diagram D)*.

3. Stabilize the weave in one of the following ways:

   Option 1: Fuse the intersections. Cut squares of fusible web smaller than the width of the fabric tubes. Place the fusible web squares between the two fabrics at each intersection. Press *(Diagram E)*.

   Option 2: Edgestitch ⅛" (3 mm) along each side of all lengthwise strips *(Diagram F)*.

Option 3: Stitch down the center of either the lengthwise or the crosswise strips with a continuous decorative stitch, using machine embroidery thread *(Diagram G)*.

Option 4: Stitch a single pattern decorative stitch at each intersection.

4. Trim weaving strips to match the paper pattern.

5. Bind the edges with bias tape.

• Cut bias strips 2" (5 cm) wide.

• Use a bias tape maker (see page 100) or press the lengthwise edges to the middle to create 1"-wide (2.5 cm-wide) bias strips.

• Insert the bobbin filled with fusible thread in the bobbin case.

• Unfold one edge of the bias tape. Meet the unfolded tape edge to the woven section, right sides together. Stitch the tape to the edge along the crease in the tape *(Diagram H)*.

• Remove the paper backing from the woven section.

• Wrap the bias tape around the edges, covering the fusible-thread stitching. Press in place. The fusible thread holds the bias tape in place until you permanently stitch it.

• Remove the bobbin filled with fusible thread and replace with a bobbin filled with all-purpose thread.

• Edgestitch along the fold, stitching from the right side of the fabric *(Diagram I)*.

Open Weaving

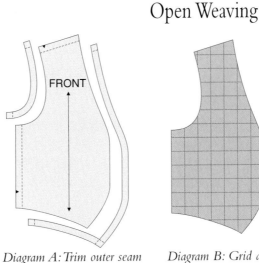

Diagram A: Trim outer seam allowances from pattern.

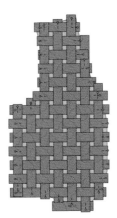

Diagram B: Grid a tissue-paper pattern.

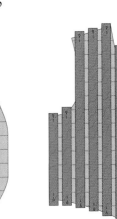

Diagram C: Pin lengthwise tubes to grid.

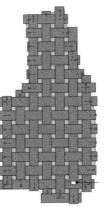

Diagram D: Weave crosswise strips and pin.

Diagram E: Fuse intersections using squares of fusible web.

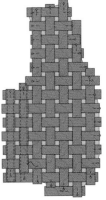

Diagram F: Edgestitch along each side of lengthwise strips.

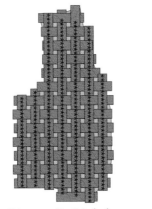

Diagram G: Stitch down lengthwise strips using a decorative stitch.

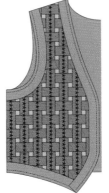

Diagram H: Stitch bias tape to garment edges.

Diagram I: Edgestitch along fold of edging.

Dimensional Weaving

Amy Bartol from Berlin, Wisconsin, created this eye-catching weaving design on the trench flaps of a blouse.

Gather Supplies

In addition to basic weaving supplies, you need:

- ❑ ¼" (6 mm) satin and metallic ribbon
- ❑ Weaving needle
- ❑ Embroidery thread or all-purpose thread

Select Weaving Elements

Choose fabric strips ¾" (2 cm) wide for the lengthwise weave and 1" (2.5 cm) wide for the crosswise weave. Amy used serged strips (see page 104) with a rolled-edge finish to make her blouse.

For the diagonal interweaving, select narrow ribbons that coordinate with the fabric strips.

Get Ready

✔ Set your machine for a straightstitch.

Create Dimensional Weaving

1. Cut out the pattern piece that the weaving will cover. Use the same fabric that you chose for the fabric strips, or use a coordinating fabric.

2. Weave the strips over the fabric base.
• Position the ¾" (2 cm) strips vertically over the base, 1" (2.5 cm) apart. Pin strips in place *(Diagram A)*.
• Add 1" (2.5 cm) horizontal strips, again 1" (2.5 cm) apart. Place these strips on top of the vertical strips, rather than weaving them in and out of the first strips. Pin strips in place *(Diagram B)*.
• Place another layer of ¾" (2 cm) strips in the 1" (2.5 cm) spaces left between the first layer of vertical strips. Place strips on top, rather than weaving them in and out. Pin strips in place *(Diagram C)*.

3. Weave ribbon through the strips.
• Using a Weaving needle, weave a length of ribbon diagonally from right to left under the first layer of vertical strips. Pin ribbons in place.
• Weave ribbons diagonally from left to right in the same manner, creating a crisscross design. Pin ribbons in place *(Diagram D)*.

4. Edgestitch the outer edges of the woven piece to secure the strips and ribbons.

Dimensional Weaving

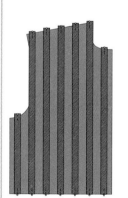

Diagram A: Pin vertical strips in place.

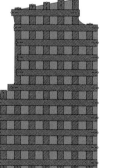

Diagram B: Place horizontal strips on top, unwoven.

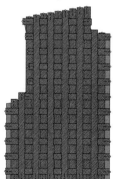

Diagram C: Place a second layer of vertical strips on top.

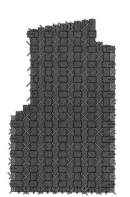

Diagram D: Weave ribbons diagonally through strips.

Pin-Weaving Variations

When you've mastered the basic strip-weaving process, try using finer yarns or threads in the lengthwise direction for a more refined look.

Gather Supplies

In addition to the basic weaving supplies, you need:
- ❏ Decorative serger threads
- ❏ Weaving needle or double-eyed needle

Select Weaving Elements

For the lengthwise section of the weaving, choose one of the threads or yarns listed under Weaving Elements on page 104.

For the crosswise sections, use a combination of yarns, threads, or fabric strips.

The pictured blouse features metallic embroidery thread (lengthwise), ⅛" (3 mm) carat braid, and ¼" (6 mm), ½" (1.3 cm) and ¾" (2 cm) Ultrasuede strips.

Create Pin-Weaving Variations

1. Position pins on a gridded surface ¼" (6 mm) or ½" (1.3 cm) apart at the top and bottom of the weaving measurement. These pins serve as the loom.

2. Anchor the beginning of the thread or yarn, then wrap the thread or yarn vertically back and forth around the pins *(Diagram)*.

3. Anchor the end of the warp (lengthwise) thread or yarn. You don't need to use fusible interfacing as a base, since the thread ends are secure.

4. Use a weaving needle to weave the crosswise strips. Add more crosswise strips to fill in the area between the pins.

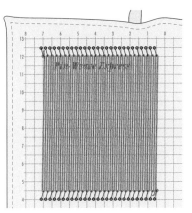

Diagram: Wrap yarn back and forth around pins.

5. Remove the pins. The weaving unit will be secure at the top and bottom edges.

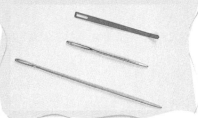

Note from Nancy

The weaving needle is a flat, large-eyed needle with a bent tip, which makes it easier to get under warp threads. The large eye handles bulky threads, yarns, or ribbons.

Enhanced Weaving

Convert a plain fabric into an eye-catcher with enhanced weaving.

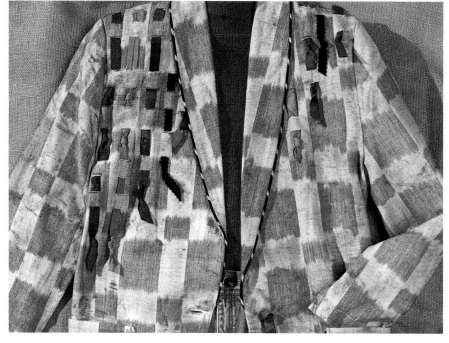

Gather Supplies

- ❑ Buttonhole cutter and block
- ❑ Buttonhole scissors
- ❑ Bodkin
- ❑ Weaving needle or double-eyed needle
- ❑ Fusible interfacing

Select Fabric

For the base fabric, choose a tightly woven fabric such as denim or canvas. The key is to use a fabric that doesn't easily ravel.

Select fabric for weaving. (See Weaving Elements on page 104.)

Create Cut Weaving

1. Determine the positions for the slits, spacing slits 1" to 3" (2.5 cm to 7.5 cm) apart. Cut ½" (1.3 cm) slits in one of the following ways.

Option 1: Use a buttonhole cutter and block. Place the fabric over the block. Cut individual slits *(Diagram A)*.

Option 2: Use buttonhole scissors to speed cutting. Fold the fabric vertically. Position the fold of the fabric in the hollowed-out opening of the buttonhole scissors *(Diagram B)*. Make one cut of the scissors, creating two parallel cuts at once. Repeat until you cut the number of columns and rows you need *(Diagram C)*.

Option 3: Use conventional scissors. Fold the fabric, mark ¼" (6 mm) lines at right angles to the fold, and cut with scissors *(Diagram D)*.

2. Use a bodkin to weave ½" (1.3 cm) strips of fabric through the cuts.

3. Knot strips for additional embellishment as illustrated *(Diagram E)*.

4. Allow some of the strip tails to be exposed if desired.

5. Back the fabric with fusible interfacing to prevent raveling.

Create Cut Weaving

Diagram A: Use a buttonhole cutter and block to cut individual slits.

Diagram B: Buttonhole scissors have a hollowed-out opening.

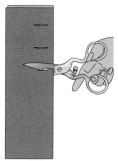

Diagram C: Cut folded fabric to make two parallel cuts at once.

Diagram D: Use conventional scissors to cut.

Diagram E: Knot woven strips if desired.

Yarn Weaving

Yarn Weaving

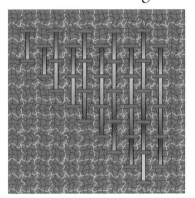

Diagram A: Make long running stitches following fabric grain.

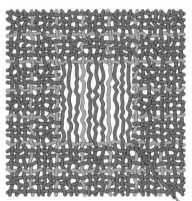

Diagram B: Carefully remove crosswise yarns between two slits.

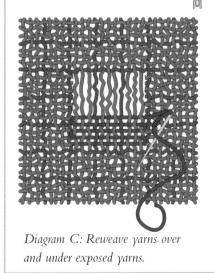

Diagram C: Reweave yarns over and under exposed yarns.

Start with fabric yardage, and then hand-stitch, reweave, remove threads, or add appliqués for special highlights.

Gather Supplies
❏ Decorative thread or yarn
❏ Large-eyed tapestry needle

Select Fabrics
These techniques involve stitching through or manipulating threads in the original fabric. Use fabrics that do not have a dense surface, such as wools, wool blends, and three-season silks. See your pattern for amount.

Create Yarn Weaving
Overstitch Fabrics Option:
1. Determine the placement of the accents on the garment or project.
2. Select a decorative thread or yarn, and use a large-eyed tapestry needle.
3. Hand-stitch through the fabric, following the lengthwise or crosswise grain. Use long running stitches to expose decorative thread *(Diagram A)*.

Note from Nancy
Add overstitching to purchased garments as well as to those you create. Overstitching gives a ready-made garment a great new look.

Unravel and Reweave Fabrics Option:
1. Determine the size and placement of the embellishment. Cut two parallel slits, following the grain line of the fabric, one at each side of the embellishment area.
2. Carefully remove the crosswise yarns between the slits *(Diagram B)*.
3. Introduce decorative yarns in the unwoven area by reweaving yarns over and under the strands of exposed yarns *(Diagram C)*.

Knit Interweaving

If you just can't bear to part with an old sweater, recycle sections of the knit to add a spectacular design element. You'll be amazed how interweaving will transform fabric!

Gather Supplies

❏ All-purpose serger thread
❏ Lightweight fusible knit interfacing
❏ Padded pressing surface
❏ Embellishment thread
❏ Weaving needle
❏ Double-eyed weaving needle (for yarns)
❏ Couture Press Cloth

Select Fabric

Choose a woven fashion fabric; see your pattern for amount.

Use a section of a recycled bulky knit sweater to match or coordinate with the woven fabric.

Get Ready

✔ Thread the two needles and the upper and lower loopers of the serger with serger thread.
✔ Set the serger for a regular overlock stitch.

Create Knit Interweaving

1. Cut a crosswise section from a bulky knit sweater.
2. Serge across the cut sections to prevent raveling.
3. Create open areas in the knit piece.
• Clip one stitch at the lengthwise edge. Drop the stitch the length of the knit piece.
• Clip stitches wherever you need a space for weaving (Diagram A).

> ### Note from Nancy
> One dropped stitch expands about four times its width. For example, using a scale of four stitches and six rows per 1" (2.5 cm), dropping one of those four stitches yields a weaving area 1" (2.5 cm) wide.

4. Cut a piece of fusible knit interfacing the size of the knit interweaving piece. Lay the interfacing, fusible side up, on a padded pressing surface. Place the knit piece on top of interfacing, with wrong side down. Pin securely in place (Diagram B).
5. Weave the raveled areas with embellishment yarns and strips of woven fabric, alternating the rows for a dramatic effect. Use a weaving needle (see page 109) to streamline the weaving process for fabric strips; use a double-eyed needle for yarns. Weave the raveled section until the open area is filled (Diagram C).

> ### Note from Nancy
> My teal dress features decorative yarns and bias strips woven in a basket weave (over two, under two). You can use an even weave (over one, under one). See Decorative Weaving, on page 104, for other weaving elements.

• Continue weaving until all open areas are filled.
6. Place a Couture Press Cloth over the knit piece and fuse to the interfacing to stabilize the shape of the inset.
7. Insert the "new" knit into your fashion garment.

Knit Interweaving

Diagram A: Clip stitches wherever you need a space for weaving.

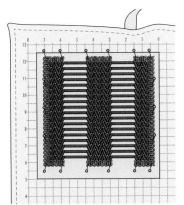

Diagram B: Pin interfacing and knit piece to padded surface.

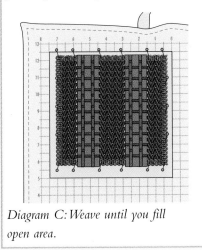

Diagram C: Weave until you fill open area.

Ultra Weave

Add dimension to your project by weaving narrow strips of Ultrasuede through the base fabric, creating a diamond design.

Gather Supplies
❑ Fine-point marker
❑ Rotary-cutting mat
❑ Buttonhole cutter
❑ Double-eyed needle or weaving needle
❑ Lightweight fusible interfacing

Select Fabric
For the base fabric, choose Ultrasuede or a tightly woven fabric.

For weaving strips, select contrasting Ultrasuede, or use ¼" (6 mm) braid, ribbons, or decorative yarns.

Create Ultra Weave
1. Draw a grid on the wrong side of the base fabric, using the fine-point marker. Prepare the grid as follows, modifying the design according to personal preference.

• Mark vertical columns 1" (2.5 cm) apart.
• Mark horizontal rows ½" (1.3 cm) apart.
• Do not mark grids in seam or hem areas (Diagram A, page 114).
2. Cut openings for the weaving.
• Place the base fabric on a rotary-cutting mat or a piece of wood.
• Beginning at the left vertical column, use a buttonhole cutter to cut a ½" (1.3 cm) vertical slit between the markings for the first and second horizontal rows.
• Skip the next horizontal row. Cut a ½" (1.3 cm) vertical slit between the markings for the third and fourth horizontal rows.
• Continue as shown, cutting slits between the alternate horizontal rows (Diagram B, page 114).
• In the second vertical column, cut slits on each side of markings in alternate rows as shown, spacing cuts ⅛" to ¼" (3 mm to 6 mm) apart (Diagram C, page 114).

- Repeat until slits are cut in the entire fabric *(Diagram D)*.

3. Weave strips through the cut openings.

- Create enhancing strips by cutting ¼" (6 mm) Ultrasuede strips. Or use braid, ribbons, or decorative yarns.

- Thread an enhancing strip through the eye of a double-eyed needle or a weaving needle. Begin at the upper left corner and weave diagonally under the slits *(Diagram E)*. Because the end of the needle is blunt, it easily passes under the slits.

- After you insert all strips from left to right, repeat the process, weaving additional strips from right to left until you have woven all rows *(Diagram F)*.

4. Cut a piece of lightweight fusible interfacing the same size as the base fabric. Fuse the interfacing to the wrong side of the woven section.

Note from Nancy

When pressing Ultrasuede, select your iron's wool setting and press from the wrong side, using a press cloth. Very light pressure prevents marring or flattening the surface of the fabric.

Time-savers

Let your children help! Ultra Weaving a cosmetic bag or a book cover is a good first project for a young person. Even if your child isn't ready to tackle the entire project, he or she can weave the strips once you've cut the slits.

Use a rotary cutter and cutting mat to cut your Ultrasuede strips. Always be sure your cutting instruments are sharp.

Making Ultra Weave

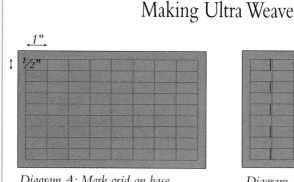

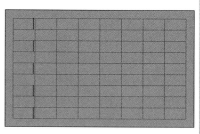

Diagram A: Mark grid on base fabric.

Diagram B: Cut vertical slits in first row.

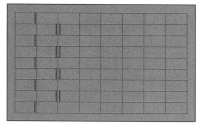

Diagram C: Cut vertical slits in second column.

Diagram D: Repeat until all slits are cut.

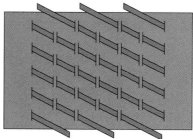

Diagram E: Weave Ultrasuede strips diagonally through slits.

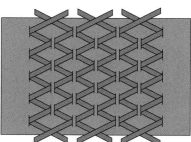

Diagram F: Weave additional strips in opposite direction.

Couched Weaving

Diagram A: Couch decorative yarns using a blindhem stitch.

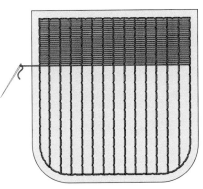

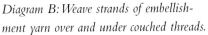

Diagram B: Weave strands of embellishment yarn over and under couched threads.

Spice up a garment by couching embellishment thread onto the surface and weaving threads through the couching.

Gather Supplies
❑ Monofilament thread
❑ All-purpose sewing thread that matches the fabric
❑ Open toe or embroidery foot
❑ Weaving needle
❑ Embellishment yarns

Select Fabrics
Choose a purchased garment, or add couched weaving to a solid-colored fabric.

Get Ready
✔ Thread the needle with monofilament thread and the bobbin with all-purpose thread.

✔ Replace the conventional foot with an open toe or embroidery foot.
✔ Adjust the sewing machine to a blindhem stitch, a medium stitch length, and a medium stitch width.

Create Couched Weaving
1. Arrange the decorative yarns vertically on the project. Space the yarns ½" to ¾" (1.3 cm to 2 cm) apart.
2. Couch or stitch the yarns to the fabric by sewing with a blindhem stitch. Line the straight part of the blindhem stitches next to the yarn and let the zigzag part of the stitches attach the yarn to the fabric. This stitching positions the yarns like the warp (lengthwise yarns) of a loom *(Diagram A)*.
3. Using a weaving or double-eyed needle, weave strands of embellishment yarns over and under the

couched threads. Varying the colors of embellishment thread adds interest to the weaving *(Diagram B)*.

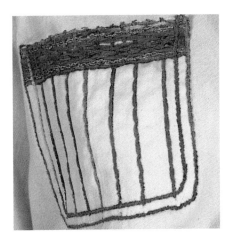

Buttonhole Weaving

Stitch a series of buttonholes along a finished edge. Then weave interesting fabric or trim, such as the bias-plaid strips featured, through those buttonholes. What an eye-catching creation!

Gather Supplies
❏ All-purpose sewing thread
❏ Buttonhole foot
❏ Bodkin or weaving needle

Select Fabrics
Choose a ready-made garment or select fashion fabric; see your pattern for amount.

Choose Ultrasuede strips, bias fabric strips, ribbon, or trim to use as weaving strips.

Get Ready
✔ Thread the sewing machine with thread to match the fashion fabric, or use contrasting thread as an accent.
✔ Replace the conventional foot with a buttonhole foot.
✔ Adjust the machine for a buttonhole stitch.

Note from Nancy
Because these buttonholes are purely decorative, this is a great place to use machine embroidery threads. If you have a computerized sewing machine, take advantage of its ability to make every buttonhole the same size.

Create Buttonhole Weaving
1. Space and stitch vertical buttonholes ½" to 1" (1.3 cm to 2.5 cm) apart and ½" (1.3 cm) from the finished edge *(Diagram A)*.
2. Weave ½" (1.3 cm) ribbon, binding, or fabric strips through the buttonholes, using a bodkin or weaving needle. Choose from a variety of methods for adding the trim: weaving *(Diagram B)*; whipstitching the outer edges *(Diagram C)*; or whipstitching with two different strands of trim, adding the second trim from the opposite direction *(Diagram D)*.

Create Buttonhole Weaving

Diagram A: Stitch buttonholes.

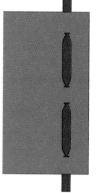

Diagram B: Weave trim through holes.

Diagram C: Whipstitch trim through holes.

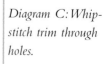

Diagram D: Whipstitch two trims through holes.

More Ideas for Textured Embellishment

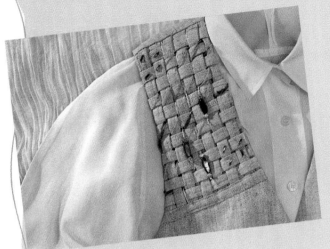

Strip Weaving, page 104
Embellish the weaving with ribbons, decorative yarns, or beads, and add as an accent to a small portion of a garment.

Dimensional Weaving, page 108
This is the blouse I'm wearing on the cover.

Yarn Weaving, page 111
A simple addition along the front dresses up a jacket.

Diamond Tucks, page 94, with Pleated Patchwork, page 82
Mix two techniques for a unique blouse.

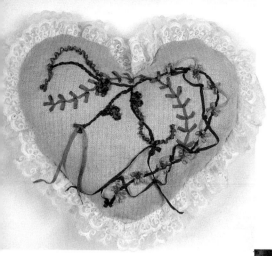

Embroider a picture-perfect Ring Bearer's Pillow *(left and page 126)*. Easy Silk-Ribbon Roses on the collar of a purchased blouse *(right and page 132)* are quick and easy to make.

Silk-ribbon embroidery adds a touch of elegance to almost any project. Now you can stitch this lovely embellishment by hand or machine.

Magical Silk Ribbon

Machine-made chainstitches *(left and page 124)* embellish a purple tunic. Compare the finished look of lazy daisy stitches *(right and page 130)* made by hand (shown on the right) and by machine (shown on the left).

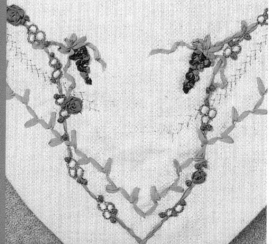

To make a stunning Silk-Ribbon Collar, combine stitches made by hand with some made by machine *(left and page 120)*.

Silk-Ribbon Collar,
page 120

Silk-Ribbon Embroidery

Use your sewing machine to stitch elegant silk-ribbon embroidery, or try traditional hand-sewing techniques.

Silk-ribbon embroidery dates back to the mid-1700s, when French royalty reserved for themselves alone the intricate designs created by hand-stitching narrow silk ribbons onto fabric.

More than two centuries later, ribbon embroidery has made a comeback, this time with a democratic slant. Instead of embellishing royal robes, silk ribbon now turns up on everything from denim to velvet, and the stitching is not restricted to handwork.

In this chapter, I show you how easily you can create this lavish embellishment, both by hand and by machine. First, I describe the supplies, fabrics, and preparations you'll need for any silk-ribbon embroidery project. In the other sections of this chapter, I show you how to create specific stitches and stitch combinations to make beautiful embellishments.

Hand Silk-Ribbon Embroidery

Gather Supplies

Additional information about materials marked with ★ follow the list.

❑ Fabric marker or pencil
❑ Tear-away stabilizer with preprinted design (optional)
❑ Fabric Pattern Transfer Kit (optional)
❑ Hand embroidery hoop with an adjustable tension screw
❑ Hand-sewing needles★
❑ Silk ribbon★
❑ Stiletto
❑ Embroidery floss or pearl cotton (for roses)

Silk ribbon comes in a variety of widths, ranging from a narrow 2 mm (approximately ¹⁄₁₆"), to 4 mm (⅛"), 7 mm (¼"), and 13 mm (½").

As an alternative, cut silk fabric into narrow bias strips to make ribbons. You can embroider with ribbons as wide as 1¼" or 1½" (32 mm or 38 mm).

Hand-sewing needles used with silk ribbon must have an eye large enough that the ribbon remains flat, not folded or crumpled. Needles designed especially for silk-ribbon embroidery are available in a full range of sizes that correspond to ribbon width and are

suited for a variety of ribbon widths. Crewel needles, sizes 5/10, also have large eyes appropriate for ribbon embroidery.

Select Fabrics

Choose fabrics with a medium weave, such as linen or linenlike fabrics. Evenweave fabric, available at needlework shops and some fabric stores, is specifically designed for ribbon embroidery. This 100% cotton fabric has a tight, flat weave, so knots and backstitches won't show through.

Get Ready

✔ Mark the design on the fabric in one of three ways:

• Use a fabric marker or pencil.

• Purchase designs preprinted on tear-away stabilizer. Position the stabilizer on the fabric and pin in place. Once you complete the embroidery, gently tear away the stabilizer.

• Use a Fabric Pattern Transfer Kit.

✔ Set up the hoop.

• Place the smaller hoop on a table, and position the fabric over the top of the hoop, right side up.

• Place the larger hoop over the fabric; tighten the screw until the hoop holds the fabric taut. The fabric should be even with the top edge of the hoop *(Diagram A)*.

✔ Cut a 14" to 16" (35.5 cm to 40.5 cm) length of ribbon, cutting the ends at a diagonal. Longer lengths often fray or shred.

✔ Thread the needle by inserting the diagonal end of the ribbon through the eye of the needle.

✔ Secure the ribbon end as follows. Insert the needle ¼" (6 mm) from the end of the ribbon *(Diagram B)*. Pull the opposite end of the ribbon, bringing the pierced end closer to the needle eye *(Diagram C)*. Slip the ribbon end over the needle eye, cinching the ribbon end against the needle *(Diagram D)*.

✔ Tie a soft knot on the opposite end of the ribbon by folding the ribbon ¼" (6 mm) from the end and inserting the needle through the folded section *(Diagram E)*. Gently pull the ribbon through the end stitch, forming a soft knot. Do not pull the knot tight.

Hand Silk-Ribbon Embroidery

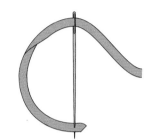

Diagram A: Place fabric even with top of embroidery hoop.

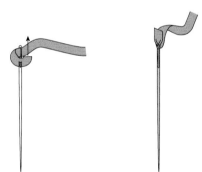

Diagram B: Pierce ribbon ¼" from end.

Diagram C: Pull opposite end of ribbon.

Diagram D: Slip ribbon end over needle eye.

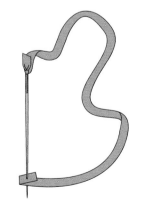

Diagram E: Fold ribbon and insert needle through fold.

Machine Silk-Ribbon Embroidery

Gather Supplies
- ❑ Metafil or machine embroidery needle
- ❑ Monofilament nylon thread
- ❑ Lingerie/bobbin thread
- ❑ Spring tension hoop
- ❑ Fabric marker or pencil
- ❑ Fabric Pattern Transfer Kit (optional)
- ❑ Silk ribbon
- ❑ Stiletto or Trolley Needle
- ❑ Light- to medium-weight interfacing

Select Fabric
Choose any type of fabric; you have no fabric limitations.

Back the fabric with interfacing.

Get Ready
- ✔ Insert a Metafil needle or a machine embroidery needle. This type of needle has a larger eye than a universal needle and a specially designed needle scarf, ideal when working with filament threads.
- ✔ Thread the needle of the machine with monofilament thread. This special thread is virtually invisible on a completed project.

Note from Nancy
Position the thread on your machine so that it unwinds from the top down. The thread feeds through the machine more smoothly in this direction. If your machine has a horizontal thread spindle, place the top of the spool on the spindle first so that the bottom of the spool faces to the left (Diagram A).

- ✔ Fill the bobbin with lingerie/bobbin thread. A special twist in this thread creates some stretch as you sew. This stretch draws the top thread to the underside of the fabric, adding dimension to the design.
- ✔ Remove the presser foot.
- ✔ Lower or cover the feed dogs.
- ✔ Loosen the top tension by two numbers or positions. (For example, adjust the tension from 5 to 3.)
- ✔ Set up the hoop.
- • Place the larger spring tension hoop down first, and position the fabric over the top of the hoop, right side up.
- • Place the smaller hoop inside the larger hoop so that the fabric is taut and is even with the bottom of the hoop *(Diagram B)*.

Machine Silk-Ribbon

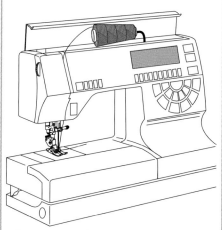

Diagram A: Place spool on machine so that spool bottom faces left.

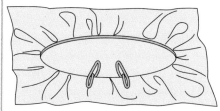

Diagram B: Place fabric even with bottom of embroidery hoop.

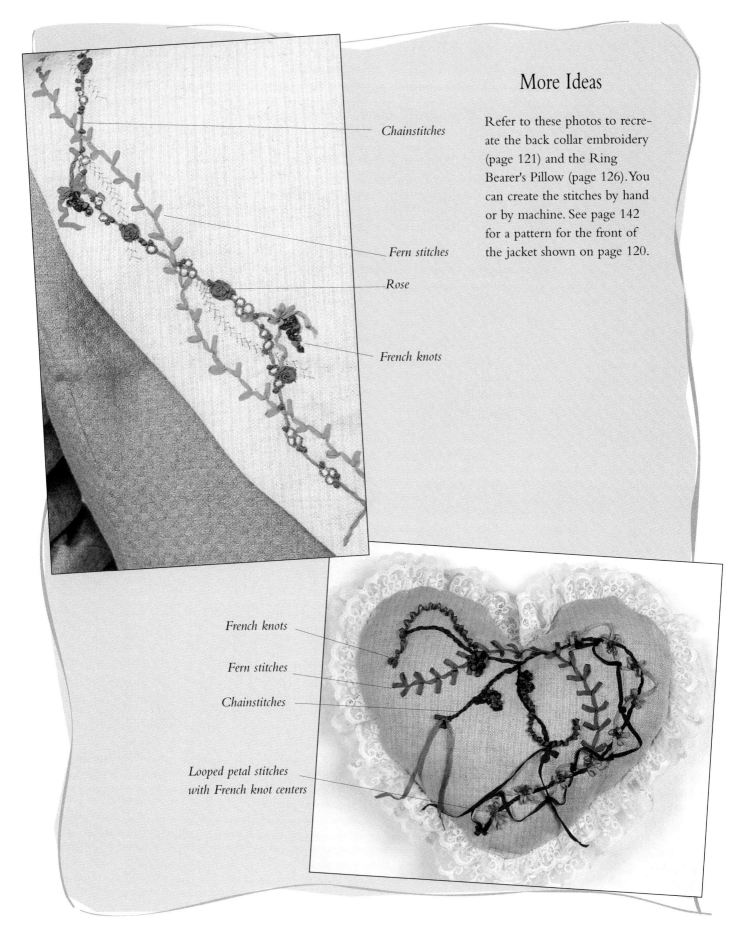

More Ideas

Refer to these photos to recreate the back collar embroidery (page 121) and the Ring Bearer's Pillow (page 126). You can create the stitches by hand or by machine. See page 142 for a pattern for the front of the jacket shown on page 120.

Chainstitches

Fern stitches

Rose

French knots

French knots

Fern stitches

Chainstitches

Looped petal stitches with French knot centers

Chainstitch

The purple tunic showcases basic silk-ribbon chainstitch.

Create Hand Chainstitch

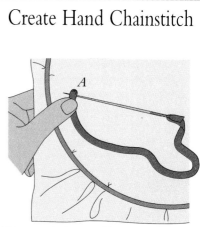

Diagram A: Bring ribbon up through fabric at A, design starting point.

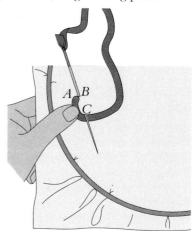

Diagram B: Insert needle at B and bring out at C, top of chainstitch.

You'll be amazed at how simple it is to create this stitch either by hand or by machine, and how easily either technique adds interest to fabric.

Create Hand Chainstitch

1. Bring the ribbon up through the fabric at A, the starting point for the design *(Diagram A)*. Fluff and straighten the ribbon with the side of the needle, a stiletto, or your fingers.

2. Form a ¼" to ½" (6 mm to 13 mm) loop with the ribbon. Hold the ribbon flat with your free thumb.

3. Insert the needle at B, directly to the side of the starting point. Bring it out again at C, the top of the stitch *(Diagram B)*. Pull the ribbon through the fabric. Don't pull it too taut; let it relax and form a natural curve.

4. Repeat, starting the next chain-stitch at the top of the previous chainstitch *(Diagram C)*.

Note from Nancy
Keep the ribbon relaxed and flat as you stitch. If you pull it tight or let the ribbon twist too much, your stitches won't look like chainstitches. Practice on a scrap to get the feel for this stitch.

Note from Nancy
Your ribbon may twist and tangle after several stitches. Periodically let the ribbon relax and untangle by inverting the hoop and letting the ribbon hang free until it untwists.

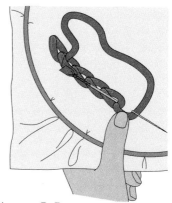

Diagram C: Repeat, starting next chainstitch at top of previous stitch.

Create Machine Chainstitch

Note: Use steps 1 through 3 for any silk-ribbon machine-embroidery stitch.

1. Draw a line on the fabric with a fabric marking pen or pencil, indicating the position for the stitches. Position the hoop so that the first stitch is under the needle.

2. Make the first stitch.

• Hold the machine's top thread taut in one hand. Turn the flywheel by hand to sew one stitch, drawing up the bobbin thread. Bring both threads to the back of the machine *(Diagram A)*.

• Lower the presser bar to sewing or embroidery position *(Diagram B)*. This is very important! Since you're stitching without a presser foot, you may have a hard time determining if the bar is up or down. Always check. If you don't lower the bar, you'll end up with a tangled thread mass on the wrong side of the fabric.

3. Sew in place several times at the top of the design to lock stitches. Cut off excess thread tails.

4. Cut a length of ribbon twice the length needed for the chain design. One of the advantages of doing embroidery on the sewing machine over hand embroidery is that you can work with longer lengths of ribbon.

5. Place the center of the ribbon horizontally on the fabric at the starting point. Stitch back and forth over the ribbon several times *(A)*. Stop with the needle out of the fabric. This is called a tackstitch *(Diagram C)*.

6. Move the fabric the length desired for one chainstitch. Place the needle down in the fabric. Cross the ribbons in front of the needle, allowing a slight amount of slack *(Diagram D)*. Tackstitch at B, over the crossed ribbons *(Diagram E)*.

7. Repeat, chainstitching along the remainder of the design *(Diagram F)*. Experiment, changing the length of individual chainstitches to create different looks.

Machine

Hand

Create Machine Chainstitch

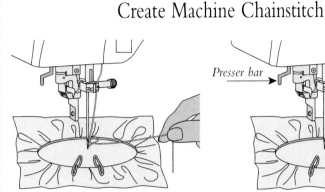

Diagram A: Draw bobbin thread through fabric and pull both threads to back.

Diagram B: Lower presser bar to sewing or embroidery position.

Presser bar

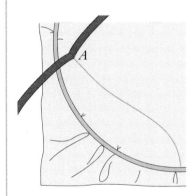

Diagram C: Tackstitch center of ribbon.

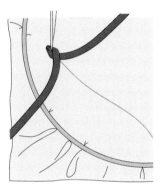

Diagram D: Cross ribbons in front of needle.

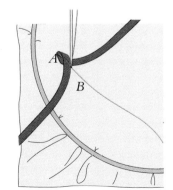

Diagram E: Tackstitch over crossed ribbons.

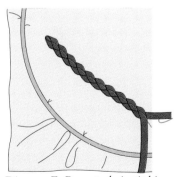

Diagram F: Repeat, chainstitching along remainder of design.

Fern Stitch

Fern stitches, which have three leaves that are all the same length, form the green vine of this Ring Bearer's Pillow.

Create Hand Fern Stitch

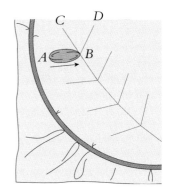

Diagram A: Bring needle up at A (leaf tip) and insert at B (center).

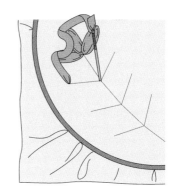

Diagram B: Pull ribbon through fabric.

In the late nineteenth century, Victorian stitchers made silk-ribbon embroidery popular by using it in their highly embellished crazy quilts and other projects. Since flowers and other items from nature were among the Victorians' most popular motifs, fern stitches made great stems and background foliage.

Create Hand Fern Stitch

1. Draw your design on fabric using a fabric marker or pencil. Make all three leaves (left, center, and right) the same length.

Note from Nancy
Consider drawing only a few complete ferns. After stitching several ferns, you can use your judgment to determine placement of the side stitches. Then you may draw only the base line, filling in the rest of the leaves as you stitch.

2. Start at the top of the design. Bring the needle up at the tip of the left leaf *(A)*, and insert the needle at the center point *(B) (Diagram A)*. Pull the ribbon through the fabric, placing a finger under the loop. Fluff and straighten the ribbon before completing the stitch. Do not pull the ribbon taut; allow it to have a little slack *(Diagram B)*.

3. Bring the needle up at C, the top of the center leaf, and then down again at B, the center point.

4. Bring the needle up at D, the tip of the right leaf, and then down again at B, the center point, to complete one fern stitch. Straighten and fluff the ribbon.

5. Repeat the three-step stitching process for each fern stitch, making the tip of each subsequent outer leaf a fraction below the center point of the previous stitch *(Diagram C)*.

Diagram C: Begin each new outer leaf a fraction below center of previous stitch.

Create Machine Fern Stitch

1. Cut the ribbon twice the length needed for your design.

2. Place the end of the ribbon on the fabric ½" (1.3 cm) below the tip of the center leaf. Most of the ribbon extends above the line. Tackstitch at A, the tip of the center leaf *(Diagram A)*.

3. Fold the ribbon down on top of itself, concealing the tackstitch. Move the hoop slightly to either side of the ribbon, and stitch alongside the ribbon to the base of the leaf. This is called a walkstitch. Tackstitch at B, the base of the leaf *(Diagram B)*.

4. Angle the ribbon along the left leaf line and walkstitch alongside the ribbon. Tackstitch at C, the tip of the left leaf *(Diagram C)*.

5. Fold the ribbon back on itself and walkstitch back to B, the center. Tackstitch *(Diagram D)*.

6. Repeat for the right leaf *(Diagram E)*.

7. Complete additional fern stitches in the same manner by tacking, folding, and walkstitching *(Diagram F)*.

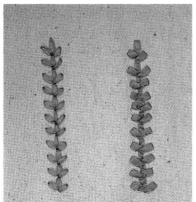

Hand   *Machine*

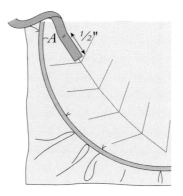

Diagram A: Tackstitch at A, tip of center leaf.

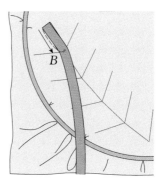

Diagram B: Walkstitch beside folded ribbon; tackstitch at B, leaf center.

Diagram C: Walkstitch along left leaf; tackstitch at C, tip of leaf.

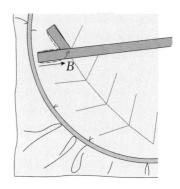

Diagram D: Walkstitch back to center; tackstitch at B.

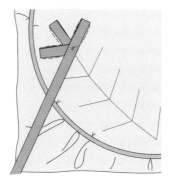

Diagram E: Repeat walkstitching and tackstitching for right leaf.

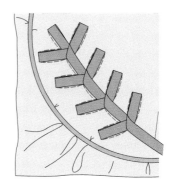

Diagram F: Completed machine fern stitches.

French Knots

French knots may be small details, but they add interest and dimension to a garment.

My jacket collar features both hand- and machine-stitched French knots. I used them in clustered groups and as individual stitches. For a special accent, make French knots using two ribbons of different colors.

Create Hand French Knots

1. Bring the needle up at A, the position for the knot. Pull the ribbon taut with your free hand.

2. Wrap the ribbon around the tip of the needle two to four times *(Diagram A)*. Wrap as close to the fabric as you can and still get the needle back through the fabric. I usually wrap the needle two or three times. More wraps make a larger knot.

3. Insert the needle at B, next to the beginning stitch, and pull the ribbon through the fabric *(Diagram B)*.

Create Hand French Knots

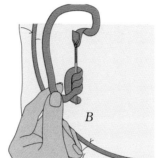

Diagram A: Wrap ribbon around needle tip two to four times.

Diagram B: Insert needle at B, next to first stitch.

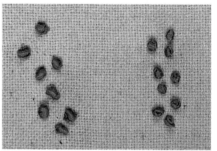

Machine   *Hand*

Create Machine French Knots

1. Place the ribbon end on the fabric at the position for the knot and tackstitch. Stop stitching with the needle in the fabric.

2. Wrap the ribbon around the machine needle two to four times. Slightly relax the tension on the ribbon, allowing it to stand free of the needle *(Diagram A)*. Hold the ribbon around the needle with a stiletto, a trolley needle, a small screwdriver, or your fingers.

3. Make two tackstitches, stitching out of the center and then back into the center twice *(Diagram B)*.

4. Complete your French knot or French knot cluster.

• For a single French knot, clip the ribbon close to the tackstitch, and secure the ends with several machine stitches *(Diagram C)*.

• For a French knot cluster, after you finish the first knot, walkstitch to the position for the second knot. Repeat steps 1 through 3 until you've made all the knots. Complete the final knot the same as for a single French knot.

Create Machine French Knots

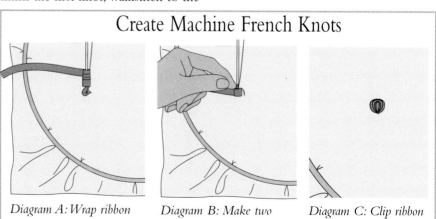

Diagram A: Wrap ribbon around machine needle two to four times.

Diagram B: Make two tackstitches into and out of French knot center.

Diagram C: Clip ribbon close to tackstitches; secure ends with machine stitches.

Create French Knot Variations

Two-tone French Knots: Use two ribbons of different colors. Tack both lengths to the fabric, and treat them as a single ribbon when wrapping and stitching the knot *(Diagram D)*.

Draped French Knots: Complete one French knot and then walkstitch to the position for the second knot, letting the ribbon drape between the two stitches. Stitch another knot; repeat *(Diagram E)*.

Note from Nancy
To reduce bulk in your silk-ribbon project, don't knot each ribbon. Instead, weave ribbon ends under previously sewn stitches on the back of the fabric.

Create French Knot Variations

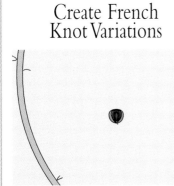

Diagram D: To make two-tone French knot, use two ribbons of different colors.

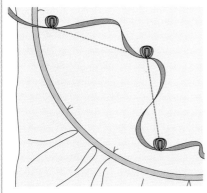

Diagram E: To make draped French knots, let ribbon drape between stitches.

Bullion Stitches

Make bullion stitches almost exactly like you make French knots. Although the technique is similar, the result is a larger and longer stitch. You can use bullion stitches to form rosebuds.

Create Hand Bullion Stitches

Follow the directions for a hand French knot, except wrap the ribbon six or more times around the needle. Then insert the needle ¼" (6 mm) away from the beginning stitch, and pull the ribbon through the fabric. Spread the ribbon to fill in the area.

Create Machine Bullion Stitches

Follow the directions for a machine French knot, except wrap the ribbon around the needle six to ten times. Tackstitch ¼" (6 mm) away from center of knot, and spread the ribbon to fill in the area.

Hand   Machine

Lazy Daisy Stitch

*Now that you're familiar with basic stitches for stems and leaves,
you can add beautiful floral highlights by altering these stitches.*

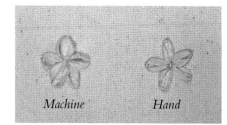

Machine   *Hand*

Create Hand Lazy Daisy Stitch

1. Use a fabric marking pen or pencil to draw the daisy petals on the fabric.
2. Bring the needle and ribbon up through the fabric at A, the center of the flower.
3. Form a loop the size of the petal.
4. Insert the needle at B, close to the starting point, and bring it up at C, the inner edge of the loop's crest *(Diagram A)*. Pull the ribbon through.
5. Insert the needle at D, the loop's outer edge, and then bring it up again at A, the flower center *(Diagram B)*.
6. Repeat steps 1 through 5 until you complete all petals.

Create Machine Lazy Daisy Stitch

1. Tackstitch the end of the ribbon at the daisy center. Stop with the needle in the fabric and clip thread tails.
2. Walkstitch to the tip of a petal *(Diagram C)*.
3. Gently wrap the ribbon around the needle without pulling it tight.
4. At petal tip, tackstitch over ribbon several times, ending with the needle in front of the ribbon *(Diagram D)*.
5. Walkstitch to the flower center, and tackstitch the ribbon to form a petal *(Diagram E)*.
6. Repeat to form five daisy petals.

Fuchsia: To make a fuchsia, form three to five lazy daisy stitches radiating from a center point. Use a second color ribbon to make three lazy daisy stitches pointing down. These are the blooms. Add stamen and pistils with straightstitches and French knots *(Diagram F)*. Use embroidery floss or smaller ribbon for the stamen and pistils.

Create Machine Lazy Daisy Stitch

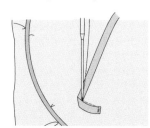

Diagram C: Tackstitch ribbon at flower center; walkstitch to petal tip.

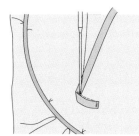

Diagram D: Tackstitch over ribbon at petal tip.

Diagram E: Walkstitch to center; tackstitch to form petal.

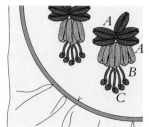

Diagram F: Make fuschia with lazy daisy stitches (A), straightstitches (B), and French knots (C).

Create Hand Lazy Daisy Stitch

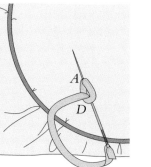

Diagram A: Bring needle up at A (center); insert at B; bring out at C (tip).

Diagram B: Insert needle at D (loop outer edge); bring up at A (center).

Looped Petal Stitch

For a free-form flower, try making looped petal stitches.

Machine   Hand

Use 4 mm silk ribbon or choose wider 7 mm ribbon, as I did, to make the looped petal stitch.

Create Hand Looped Petal Stitch

1. Bring the needle and ribbon up through the fabric at flower center. Fluff the ribbon with the point of the needle to keep ribbon from bunching at the opening.

2. Form a loop. Hold the loop with your free thumb so the ribbon folds back on itself without twisting.

3. Insert the needle slightly above the starting point, piercing the ribbon *(Diagram A)*.

4. Repeat to form additional petals as desired *(Diagram B)*.

5. If desired, add French knots to the flower center.

Create Machine Looped Petal Stitch

1. Tackstitch the ribbon end at the flower center.

2. Loop the ribbon to form a petal. Use a stiletto, a trolley needle, a screwdriver, or a toothpick to hold the end of the loop in place. Tackstitch at the flower center *(Diagram C)*.

3. Rotate the hoop slightly and repeat the loop-and-tackstitch sequence until you complete the flower.

4. Finish the stitches.

• For a single flower, cut the ribbon at the center after completing the flower, and tackstitch over the end of the ribbon *(Diagram D)*.

• For a series of flowers, walkstitch the needle to the position for the next flower, allowing the ribbon to drape gracefully between flowers. Repeat steps 1 through 3 to form additional flowers *(Diagram E)*. Finish off the final flower as you would a single flower.

Note from Nancy
When working with wider ribbon, slightly pinch or gather the ribbon in the flower center to create a more realistic bloom.

Create Machine Looped Petal Stitch

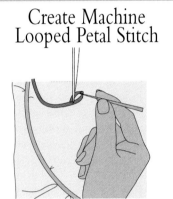

Diagram C: Use stiletto or trolley needle to hold loop while you tackstitch center.

Diagram D: Cut ribbon at flower center; tackstitch over ribbon end.

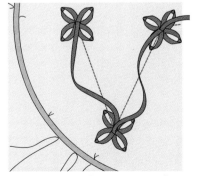

Diagram E: For flower series, walkstitch between each, letting ribbon drape.

Create Hand Looped Petal Stitch

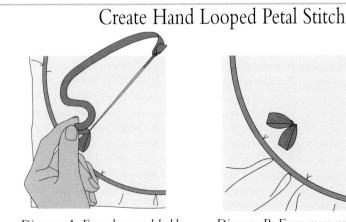

Diagram A: Form loop and hold with your free hand.

Diagram B: Form more petals as desired, pulling ribbon through fabric carefully.

Silk-Ribbon Roses

Once you master basic silk-ribbon stitches, you'll be amazed at the interesting variations you can sew.

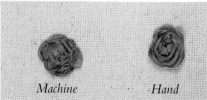

Machine   *Hand*

Make a rose collar like mine by combining stitches and techniques you've already learned with other easy stitches. The rose on this collar is called a spiderweb rose.

Create Hand Silk-Ribbon Roses

1. Use embroidery floss or pearl cotton to make a fly stitch. The fly stitch is the anchor for your rose.
• Bring the needle up at A *(Diagram A)*.
• Take the needle down at B and bring it back up at C, keeping the

needle tip over the thread.
• Take the needle down at D, completing the fly stitch. Do not finish off.
2. Still using floss or pearl cotton, add a stitch to each side of the fly stitch to make five spokes *(Diagram B)*. Finish off.
3. With silk ribbon, bring the needle up in the center of the spokes *(Diagram C)*.
4. Working in a counterclockwise direction, weave the ribbon over and under the spokes *(Diagram D)*. Keep the ribbon loose and let it twist as you work. Continue weaving until you completely cover all the spokes.

Create Hand Silk-Ribbon Roses

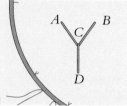

Diagram A: To make fly stitch, bring needle up at A, down at B, up at C, and down at D.

Diagram B: Add one stitch to each side of fly stitch.

Diagram C: Bring ribbon up at center of spokes.

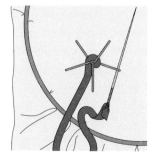

Diagram D: Weave over and under spokes in counterclockwise direction.

Create Machine Silk-Ribbon Roses

1. Mark three dots in a triangle about ¼" (6 mm) apart *(Diagram A)*.

2. Place the center of the ribbon over any dot and tackstitch in place *(Diagram B)*.

3. Hold the ribbon out of the way and walkstitch to the next dot, stopping with the needle in the fabric *(Diagram C)*.

4. Make the first round of the rose.

• Cross the ribbons in front of the needle, leaving a little slack *(Diagram D)*. Tackstitch over the crossed ribbons *(Diagram E)*.

• Walkstitch to the third dot, cross the ribbons in front of the needle, and tackstitch.

5. Continue working around the triangle in this manner, making sure your stitches don't cross at the same points *(Diagram F)*. By staggering the points where the stitches cross, you can avoid a square-looking rose.

Multicolored Rose: To make a shaded or multicolored rose, use two colors of silk ribbon. Anchor the ends at the starting point *(Diagram G)*. Work around the triangle in the same manner as for silk-ribbon roses, treating the two ribbons as one *(Diagram H)*.

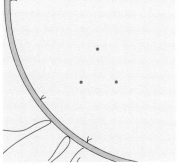

Diagram A: Draw three dots in triangle about ¼" apart.

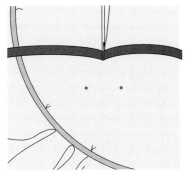

Diagram B: Tackstitch ribbon center at any dot.

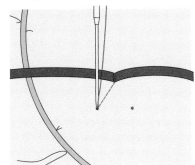

Diagram C: Walkstitch to next dot; stop with needle in fabric.

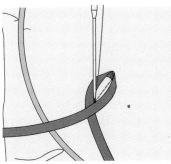

Diagram D: Cross ribbons loosely in front of needle.

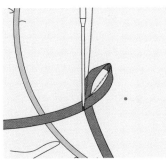

Diagram E: Tackstitch over crossed ribbons.

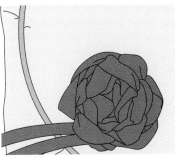

Diagram F: Continue working around triangle until rose is complete.

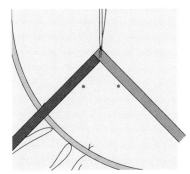

Diagram G: To make multicolored rose, tackstitch ends of two colors of ribbon at rose starting point.

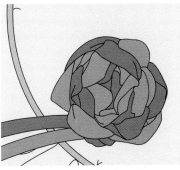

Diagram H: Completed machine multicolored rose.

Celtic Surface Texture

Instructions for Celtic Surface Texture begin on page 102.

Sashiko

Instructions for Sashiko stitching begin on page 32. Use only part of this pattern, or repeat it to cover whatever size area you wish to stitch.

Monograms

Instructions for Monograms begin on page 44.

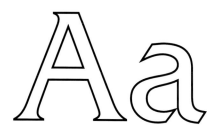  

  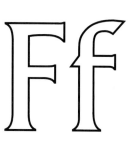

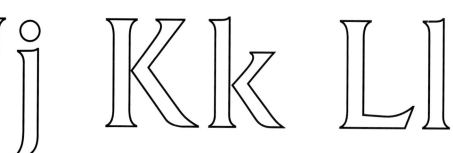

Oo Pp
Qq Rr Ss
Tt Uu Vv
Ww Xx
Yy Zz

Upper left

Upper right

Battenberg
Leaves

Instructions for Pseudo Battenberg begin on page 36. I've labeled these patterns as they appear in the photo on page 36, but you can rearrange them to fit your garment.

Lower left

Morning Star Appliqué

Instructions for Invisibly Stitched Quilt Appliqué, which begin on page 42, feature a floral vine made by adapting Morning Star appliqué. See the photo on page 42 for placement. I used single diamonds for leaves and buds, and made flowers by putting together three, four, and six of the diamonds.

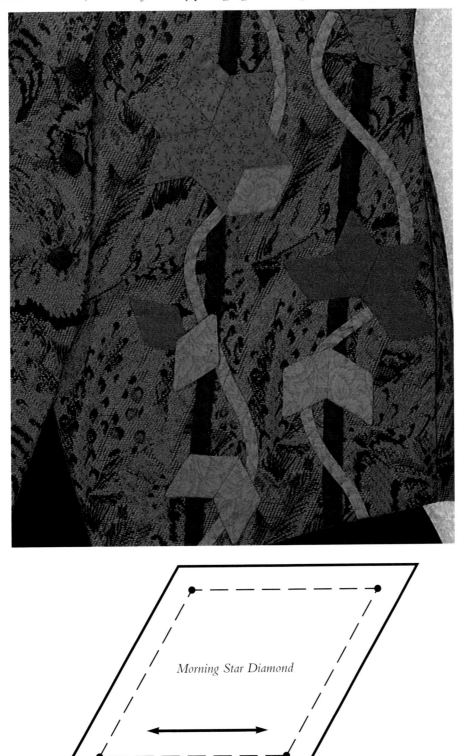

Morning Star Diamond

Sunbonnet Sue

Instructions for Invisibly Stitched Appliqué, which begin on page 40, feature a Sunbonnet Sue motif on a child's jumper. Choose your favorite Sunbonnet Sue design or use this one.

To reduce or enlarge this (or any pattern in this book), photocopy it at the appropriate percentage.

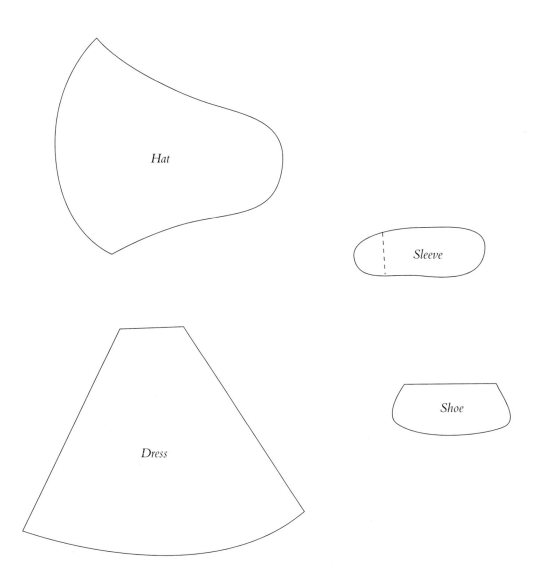

Cutwork Appliqué

Instructions for Cutwork Appliqué begin on page 54.

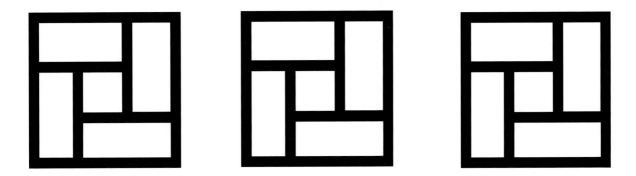

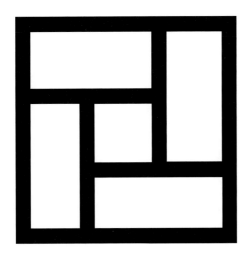

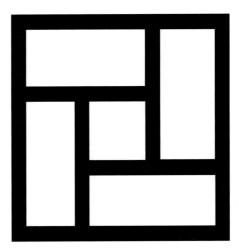

Bias Surface Texture

Instructions for Bias Surface Texture begin on page 100.

Silk-Ribbon Collar

Photos of the Silk-Ribbon Collar appear on pages 119, 120, 121, and 123. The stitches used are in the chapter, "Magical Silk Ribbon," which begins on page 118.

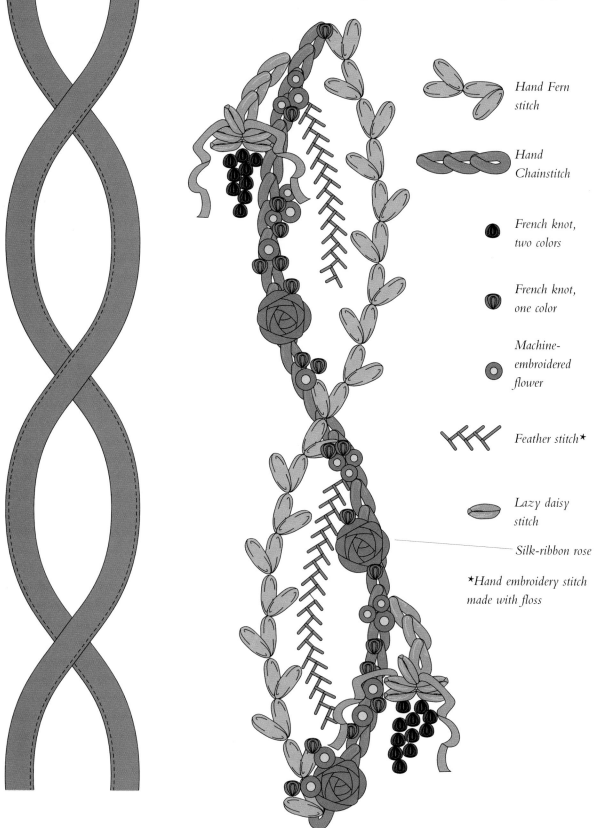

Hand Fern stitch

Hand Chainstitch

French knot, two colors

French knot, one color

Machine-embroidered flower

Feather stitch★

Lazy daisy stitch

Silk-ribbon rose

★*Hand embroidery stitch made with floss*

Ring Bearer's Pillow

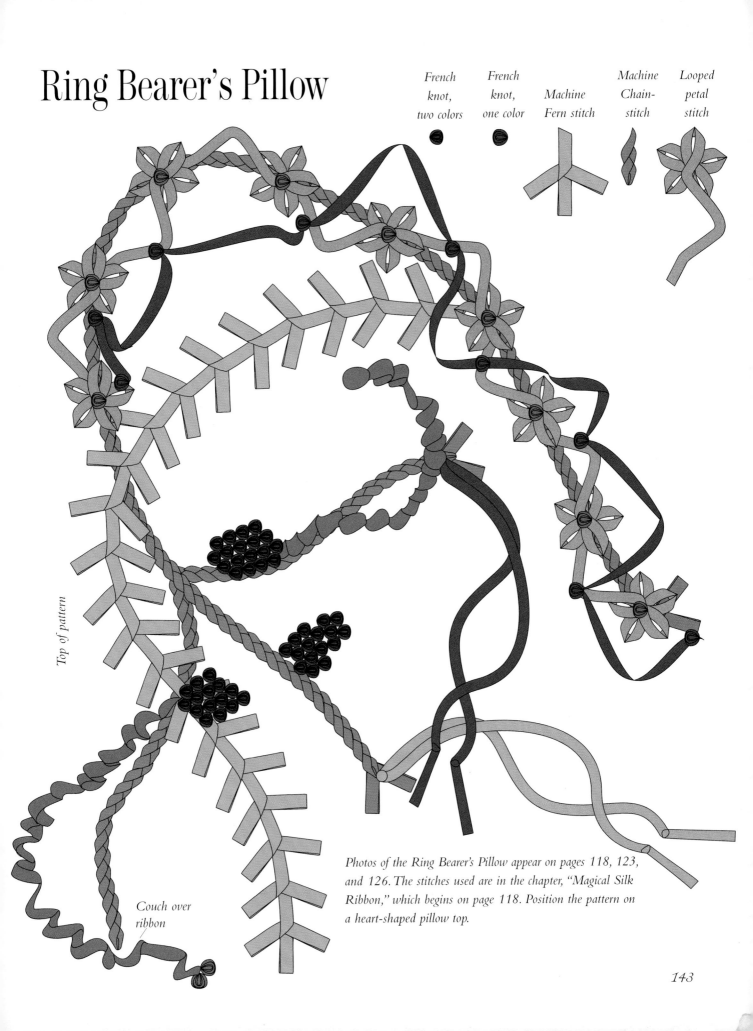

French knot, two colors

French knot, one color

Machine Fern stitch

Machine Chain-stitch

Looped petal stitch

Top of pattern

Couch over ribbon

Photos of the Ring Bearer's Pillow appear on pages 118, 123, and 126. The stitches used are in the chapter, "Magical Silk Ribbon," which begins on page 118. Position the pattern on a heart-shaped pillow top.

Nancy Zieman—businesswoman, home economist, and national sewing authority—is the producer and hostess of the popular show "Sewing With Nancy," which appears exclusively on public television stations. The show, broadcast since September 1982, is the longest-airing sewing program on television. Nancy organizes each show in a how-to format, concentrating on step-by-step instructions.

Nancy also produces and hosts *Sewing With Nancy* videos. Each video contains three segments from her television program. Currently, there are 28 one-hour videos available to retailers, educators, libraries, and sewing groups.

In addition, Nancy is founder and president of Nancy's Notions, which publishes *Nancy's Notions Sewing Catalog*. This large catalog contains more than 4,000 products, including sewing books, notions, videos, and fabrics.

Nancy has written several books including: *Fitting Finesse*, *501 Sewing Hints*, and *Sewing Express*. In each book, Nancy emphasizes efficient sewing techniques that produce professional results.

Nancy was named the 1988 Entrepreneurial Woman of the Year by the Wisconsin Women Entrepreneurs Association. In 1991, she also received the National 4-H Alumni Award. She is a member of the American Association of Family and Consumer Sciences and the American Home Sewing & Crafts Association.

Nancy lives in Beaver Dam, Wisconsin, with her husband and business partner, Rich, and their two sons, Ted and Tom.